© 2018 Lisa Grazan

All rights reserved. No part of this book may be reproduced in any form or by any electronic or mechanical means, including information storage and retrieval systems, without permission in writing from the author. For information, contact Lisa Grazan at lgrazan@verizon.net.

The content of this book is for general instruction only. Each person's physical, emotional, and spiritual condition is unique. The instruction in this book is not intended to replace or interrupt the reader's relationship with a physician or other professional. Please consult your doctor for matters pertaining to your specific health and diet.

All rights reserved. No part of this publication may be reproduced, distributed, or transmitted in any form or by any means, including photocopying, recording, or other electronic or mechanical methods, without the prior written permission of the publisher or author, except in the case of brief quotations embodied in critical reviews and certain other noncommercial uses permitted by copyright law. For permission requests, email the author at lgrazan@verizon.net.

ISBN: 978-0-578-58173-6

PRINTED IN THE UNITED STATES OF AMERICA

The 5 Wellness Archetypes:
Reveal Your Personality, Master Your Health

By: Lisa Grazan

FOR MY PARENTS

TO MY MOTHER: You are the epitome of strength and grace

TO MY FATHER: Your light shines the brightest of anyone I have ever known

TABLE OF CONTENTS

10	**OPENING STATEMENT**
12	**INTRODUCTION PART I: SETTING THE STAGE**
15	**INTRODUCTION PART II: UNLEASHING MY SECRET IDENTITY**
21	**WELLNESS MANIFESTO**
23	**WELLNESS ARCHETYPE QUIZ**
	THE ELEMENTS:
28	*THE VISIONARY - SPACE*
44	*THE ARTIST - AIR*
61	*THE TRANSFORMER - FIRE*
78	*THE PACIFIST - WATER*
96	*THE ROCK - EARTH*
113	**CONCLUSION**

Opening Statement

Knowing your predominant element is like discovering your life's blueprint. It is the key to successfully creating a happy, healthy and balanced life for yourself.

As I was preparing for my first jury trial over 25 years ago, I stumbled upon a small – but what turned out to be very significant – book as I was perusing the shelves of a legal stationery store across the street from my law office. The book was aptly titled The First Trial and, at that early stage in my legal career, I thought I struck gold when I found it inconspicuously wedged between a book on Real Property and a box of extra-large binder clips. As a young attorney with only a couple weeks before my first trial date, I was seeking out any resource I could find to improve my skills.

While insatiably speed-reading through the chapter entitled "Curtain Up: The Opening Statement" my eyes were magnetized to the words of wisdom that jumped off the page and imprinted themselves indelibly in my mind: "The jury will never listen to you, or to anybody else, more closely than they will listen to the first twenty-five words out of your mouth. Do not waste them."[1] Ergo (to use some legalese) my opening remarks above in bold.

I can't help but consider this journey, dear readers, as a "trial" of sorts, making the case for adopting a more natural perspective about your health. And, while setting forth facts, presenting evidence and crafting arguments is the typical framework of any trial, never before has a verdict been so important. We spend our entire lives longing to experience that elusive "feel good zone" or peace of mind.

Yet unlike a typical trial, the ultimate goal here is not to paint a picture of good vs. bad, or right vs. wrong. It's about the process of understanding; understanding more about nature and, specifically, more about your own nature and how it directly impacts your health.

Adopting a more natural approach to your health asks you to momentarily view yourself as a collection of the natural elements themselves (Space, Air, Fire, Water, and Earth); to discover which element(s) you align with most closely; to witness how their inherent qualities uniquely manifest in your body and mind; to understand that an aggravation of those qualities leads to physical and emotional imbalance; and to know that you have the power and wherewithal to restore your own well-being either by enhancing or diminishing the qualities of those natural elements through diet and lifestyle.

In a nutshell, it's about respectfully consulting your inner nature for guidance rather than blindly surrendering to pharmaceuticals for the "answers" when you feel imbalanced. It's not a new, cutting edge perspective, mind you. It's actually ancient wisdom — tried and true — that is more relevant today than ever before.

The ideas in this book are taken from many aspects of natural healing. One of them is Ayurvedic medicine which, to me, offers the most sound and effective dietary and lifestyle recommendations of all to establish well-being. With that being said, this book is not designed as an in-depth analysis of Ayurveda. It is, however, designed to reveal your true nature and state of balance.

By the way, I won my first jury trial because I believed in my client, I knew the case inside and out, I was prepared, I paid attention to detail, and I had an unbeatable argument. Although I'm no longer in a court room, I trust in that same process here.

I certainly hope that as you read on, you'll remember more than just the first 25 words of my "opening statement." In fact, what I want you to come away with is a greater understanding of your own unique nature and the appreciation that healthy, minor adjustments can make a world of difference on your way to naturally vibrant health and emotional well-being.

Introduction Part 1: Setting the Stage

A natural approach to health and healing goes as far back for me as I can remember. It is my foundation and the only way of life I've ever known, thanks to my mother and her three sisters: my Aunt Grace, Aunt Rozella, and Aunt MaryRuth. They constantly read about yoga, exercise, alternative medicine, vitamins, nutrient content, juicing, proper food combining, and healthy cooking methods. Growing up in the late 1960's and through the 1970's in a small town outside of Pittsburgh, Pennsylvania, I didn't know anyone else who was as devoted to a naturally healthy lifestyle like my family was – or even really anyone who knew about it as much as they did. It was a lifestyle that was indoctrinated into me. At first, when I saw how different it was from the lives my friends led, I viewed it with some skepticism. Now, I recognize it as wisdom.

My mother and aunts were always immersed in books about yoga as they studied the postures' revitalizing health benefits to the joints, the glands, and the organs. I distinctly remember those weekends when I would borrow my Aunt MaryRuth's body suits and leotards, which were always too big for me, and tagged along to yoga class with them. I loved kicking my feet over my head in the Plow Pose, and I always laughed out loud when I opened my eyes wide and stuck out my tongue for Lion. Despite the enjoyment I received from wildly expressing myself, I still couldn't quite grasp the point of just sitting there with my eyes closed "watching" my breath. I "practiced" deep breathing with them, filling up my lungs and blowing it out, but I could never understand what they found so appealing about it.

I remember Aunt Grace telling me that your best sleep is before midnight and that breathing the early morning air is always better for you.

Unlike my friends' mothers, they never colored their hair but chose to go gray naturally. I remember Aunt Grace lying horizontally across her bed, and me lying next to her, our heads hanging towards the floor, as she taught me that circulation is the best-kept secret for a healthy scalp. She taught me that hanging your head over the side of your bed every night and brushing your hair 100 strokes from the nape of your neck downwards toward the ends with a natural boar-bristled hairbrush will make your hair more lustrous than any expensive salon treatment ever could.

Their make-up routine consisted of applying a little lipstick or face powder every now and then, but that was it. Instead, they had facials from a family friend who lived nearby. Helen actually made her own natural skin care products ranging from cucumber cleansing cream to mud packs and those were the only products my family used. I remember watching my aunts stand in front of a mirror and repeatedly contort their facial expressions in order to firm up the muscles which would give them a natural face lift.

My mother always stressed to me the importance of wearing clothes made from natural fibers, nothing ever polyester or synthetic. She knew the skin could "breathe" in natural fabric, but not in synthetics. It was quite a contrast to the clothes my friends wore at that time which were the latest brightly colored, form fitting, never-wrinkling styles.

They shopped at what we commonly referred to as either "Mrs. Heller's" or "The Health Store," a quaint local health food store owned by Mrs. Heller, an older woman with gray hair. Her store was in the converted basement of a big house at the end of one of downtown Greensburg's main thoroughfares. I remember walking down the flight of steps from street level where Mrs. Heller always greeted us with a smile conveying her appreciation of like-minded customers.

I remember my mom and each of my aunts buying an Acme juicer. I always drank freshly made carrot/celery/apple juice before I went to school. I also remember my mom baking whole grain bread that had an unusually dark color and a strange shape – kind of like a rectangle that collapsed at the top. I ate a slice every morning for breakfast. She always packed natural snacks in my lunch rather than candy or sugared treats like my friends had. I used to eat Tiger's Milk candy bars instead of the Choco'Lite my friends ate. I never grew up drinking soda or eating chips.

My mom and aunts actually read labels before it was fashionable to do so. I never remember eating anything canned, frozen or processed. I do remember once, however, longing for my mother to buy a frozen dinner for me to taste just to be like my friends and their families. When I finally tasted what was so popular, it was actually foreign to me — nothing like anything I had ever tasted before — not like real food at all. It was then that I realized I wasn't missing anything.

When my Aunt Rozella baked Toll House cookies, she always used carob chips in place of chocolate chips, raw honey in place of sugar, and whole grain flour in place of white flour. From a kid's perspective, though, those cookies never quite hit the sweet note I was hoping for.

My mother and aunts never took pharmaceuticals because they didn't need to. They took vitamins and other natural remedies instead. I remember opening up the old, faded cupboards in my grandmother's house to find brightly colored bottles of vitamins A, E, B Complex and Brewer's Yeast. Forget about NyQuil, Contac or Vicks VapoRub, I was "doctored" with Acerola Rose Hips lozenges if I had a cold, a spoonful of honey if I had a sore throat, or Chamomile tea if I had menstrual cramps.

Growing up, I was immersed in this natural lifestyle, but on some level, I still felt a yearning to fit in with my friends and what seemed at times like everyone else. My mother and aunts weren't like everyone else though. They marched to the beat of their own drummers. They sought a more natural approach to life and living.

Looking back now, I remember how their skin glowed, their figures were trim and strong, and their hair was lustrous. They all moved with such grace, both physically and emotionally. Sure, they had their differences among themselves and maybe disagreed with how others handled things but they all got along with everyone. I don't ever recall any trauma or drama. They navigated through their lives with grace and dignity, holding their own, holding their youth and holding their beauty. They focused on health from the inside out –long before it became popular or advised to do so. Now I can see the seeds were planted in my mind just waiting to blossom and grow.

Introduction Part 2: Unleashing My Secret Identity

As a kid I just loved watching Saturday morning cartoons. My all-time favorite was the floppy-eared canine Super Hero, Underdog, who proudly donned a long blue cape and bright red jumpsuit emblazoned with a giant capital U across his small, but mighty chest. I always smiled from ear to ear when the "humble and lovable" Shoeshine Boy exploded into his alter ego who possessed the "speed of lightning, roar of thunder, fighting all who rob and plunder!" Whenever his long, sensitive ears heard a desperate cry for help, bouncing up and down with each high-pitched plea, I loved watching him dash into a near-by phone booth and ultimately blast out revealing his secret identity to the world!

What restraint Underdog must have shown working as a shoeshine boy while knowing all the powers he possessed and all the good he could do for humankind. Those patronizing pats on his head and stingy tips from his unsuspecting customers must have left him seething. If I were in his shoes, I would be literally bursting at my seams to let everyone know just who I really was and what I could really do. I mean, after all, Underdog had the power to save the world! That's a tough one to keep under wraps.

As an adult, I still muse on Underdog because I now know how he must have felt. I clearly don't claim to possess X-ray vision or ultrasonic hearing; I don't have the wherewithal to rid the world of villains like Simon Bar Sinister or Riff Raff, and I'm certainly not equipped to take on The Marbleheads from the planet Granite, but Underdog and I still hold something special in common. You see, I too had a secret identity.

To the outside world I was an attorney. You know, someone who traffics in the "seen," relies on the facts, the hard evidence, the numbers, the signatures, the black letter law, the rules, regulations and statutes. Not only did I prepare the canvas and draw the dots, I also connected them, colored the picture and presented it to the court.

For a good chunk of my legal career I represented international "Big Pharma." I was assigned to this specific practice area because of my foreign language skills to translate German documents to determine their relevancy and privilege status. As a good attorney, I represented my clients to the best of my ability. It was my job to provide the client with the best defense possible, tearing apart the claims of injury or death from their drugs, casting doubt about any alleged side-effects, and playing up the client's "stellar" research and rigorous regulatory compliance.

Secretly, however, my job was actually ripping apart the core of my being. You see, my secret identity was a natural health advocate. I abhorred pharmaceuticals. Personally and professionally, I saw how they were dispensed like candy and yet how they could completely ravage the body. I witnessed how people put all their faith and trust in these drugs only to have their entire physiology turned upside down as their body tried desperately to fight against these invaders. It seemed like there was always some trickery involved in the drug's intent — which was to confuse the body into thinking one way, or to deceive the body into acting another way. Ultimately, the pharmaceuticals succeeded in stupefying the body's own innate intelligence as they began to break down the complex network of messaging. Well-intentioned physicians dispensed their arsenal of weapons only to sentence their patients to severe side effects while still not curing their ailments. I held absolutely no faith in Western medicine's "answer" to illness.

In my personal life I preferred natural alternatives to the allopathic approach. From my own reading and experience, I passed along to others how to use natural means to heal their body and mind and maintain their health. I knew it wasn't about taking a pill. It was about taking responsibility.

For over two decades, I was caught up in the hectic lifestyle of working as an attorney. I felt the need to sacrifice the healthy practices I once knew in the name of "just getting through the day." I thought I could catch up or make up for any deficit, but that never happened. Deadlines crowded out a full night's sleep. The workload itself took my focus away from eating well. My job responsibilities outweighed my ability to exercise, and my mind became too cluttered to even consider meditating. As the years went on, I found myself irritable all the time as I continued to run on empty. I was also on constant alert, relentlessly scanning for the next demanding email directive, or metaphorical fire to put out. Averaging four hours of sleep each night, it's no wonder my attitude and my nerves were shot. I was too wound up in hating my job to get a full night's rest and too weighed down in hating my job to wake up in the morning. After years of keeping this pace, physically I began to look tired and worn. My eyes were puffy, and my skin was dull. In fact, everything appeared dull to me. The only color I saw in my life were those red exclamation-marked emails demanding to be read immediately.

The negativity at work was pervasive. I couldn't remember the last time I had actually laughed out loud. But then again, I wasn't seeing any lightheartedness anywhere around. I was turning into someone I didn't even know and someone you would think didn't know any better.

I distinctly remember thinking to myself one day, "If this is all that life has to offer, it's just not worth it." I certainly didn't want to turn into a bitter, unhealthy, and unhappy person; but I could see that if I didn't make a radical change soon, I was well on my way to that destination. As I pondered my options, one thing kept ringing true: This isn't how I'm supposed to live my life.

It became clear to me that if I kept up this pace in my career, I was on a kamikaze mission to crash and burn. However, I was armed with a solid foundation about health, healing, diet and lifestyle and the knowledge that if you can't change your circumstances, you must change yourself. My first priority was to re-prioritize.

I adjusted and modified what I could at work. I adhered to a 9-to-5 schedule, leaving work at work. I was able to carve out time in order to reach out to my lifelines of knowledge and experience with natural medicine and healthy living as I took a deeper dive than ever before.

I became my own client and my own best advocate in search of a better life. I "hit the books" with a zeal like never before. I consulted natural medicine practitioners; studying vitamins and supplements more closely. I researched Macrobiotic and Ayurvedic healing diets and switched exclusively to organic food. I made an in-depth exploration of Yoga and put forth the concerted effort to meditate daily. I practiced gratitude; and earnestly began to "witness" my actions and mind patterns. I journaled what worked and what didn't and how I felt along the way.

As I began to emerge from the heaviness I felt, my new perspective allowed an even bigger picture to emerge around me. I had a front row seat to a play – a tragedy, no less – as I watched Act I, Act II, and Act III of the characters I was surrounded by progressively destroy their physical, mental and emotional health. Slowly but surely.

I couldn't help but notice my legal colleagues consistently consulting the vending machines for their daily fare; eating processed, frozen, microwaved, lifeless food. Now I knew what continued to fuel their physical complaints, their chronic illnesses, their jaded perspectives, and their general dissatisfaction with their jobs, their relationships, and their lives. They sat all day long staring at their computers. Downing cans of diet soda during the day and a bottle of who knows what in the evening were the norm for many of them. They complained of aches and pains, digestive upset, and migraines. They returned from their doctors with a pocket full of pills and promises but no relief.

While I had known it all along, my resurgence of natural health knowledge showed me it was their diet and lifestyle that was traveling like a freight train bound for nowhere; and it was on a fast track out of control. I wanted to scream from the top of my lungs: If you practice an unhealthy lifestyle and think you're going to correct the situation by turning to pharmaceuticals you will not regain your health!

I began to see my own efforts paying off as I felt better physically and emotionally. While I found that I could cope better at work, the truest revelation for me was that defending "Big Pharma" didn't suit me at all. Now armed with a healthy perspective and a clear mind, I realized I had to make a move.

When they say the person who represents himself has a fool for a client, it certainly wasn't true in this instance. Like any good advocate worth their weight, with their client's best interests in mind, I closely examined the facts and carefully considered all of the arguments before I came to a pivotal decision. My best advice to myself was to align with my true passion. I decided to become a natural health practitioner.

I forged a new path in my life, this time not relying on skills that were needed to fill a position but to carve out a position that needed my skills. The difference now was that I decided not to keep this part of my identity a secret any longer.

I developed a whole new client base. I could now apply my skills as a counselor to help people who were sick and tired of being sick and tired. I dispensed advice and designed strategies that my clients desperately needed. I like to say that instead of working to make my clients financially whole, I worked to make them holistically well. The bottom line is that I take great pleasure and satisfaction in educating and guiding people through the world of natural health and healing.

It still took me a while to extract myself from representing pharmaceutical clients. However, with my greater understanding of natural medicine, and my own boosted healthy body, mind and spirit, I finally decided to call it quits on representing clients that were the antithesis of who I was – the job and mindset that exhausted and eroded me.

I set my legal sights now on a different set of clients – those who have a healthy respect for nature. I have befriended and advocate for organic farmers, alternative medicine practitioners and natural food entrepreneurs.

While I'd like to analogize my "great reveal" to my favorite Super Hero bursting out of a phone booth to help those in need, I'd be short-changing myself. I have to say that the satisfaction I feel by fully embracing a healthy lifestyle that is in alignment with my core values, and using my skills and passion to counsel people who work toward a better quality of life has been much more subtle and profound for me. When you work to make yourself well you inspire and elevate so many others in the process.

While I no longer felt the need to assume a different persona to the world, the most significant revelation was to myself. I now understand what it means to "come into your own" and to "speak your truth." It's not only hitting that "sweet spot," it's like hitting that note you knew you came here to sing. It was more than just a feeling of ease and comfort. What I was finally experiencing was what they call confidence. Confidence in the message and confidence in myself as the messenger.

Wellness Manifesto

Whenever we're in physical or emotional pain we typically seek out the advice of a Western medicine practitioner. It seems to be a default reaction. Whether it's to alleviate acid reflux, ease anxiety, or recover from a broken heart, the general protocol is that physical complaints are addressed over here, and emotional matters are dealt with over there. In either instance, the typical Western approach is to match our symptoms with the current arsenal of pharmaceuticals or psychological treatments and prescribe a remedy for what's ailing us.

While the allopathic approach to healing may seem like a sound theory, it's actually a very limited, myopic and fractured view. In Western medicine's world, body and mind are considered separate systems and diet is dismissively addressed with advice like "make sure you eat right." Our complaints are being isolated, labeled, categorized and "fixed" in a vacuum. A typical Western medical approach rarely – if ever – sees us in a holistic light.

Try as it might, modern medicine just doesn't get to the root cause of our chronic problems. We may be lured by its promises of alleviating symptoms, or even "feeling great," being "more active," experiencing "more confidence" and being "happy." Consequentially, we actually find that no pill or potion will completely do the trick. Perhaps it can help us manage or even numb our physical and emotional pain, but it cannot point us to the path of true healing. This is because we're looking outside of ourselves for help. That's not the place to look.

Lasting physical and emotional healing begins by journeying inward to discover your true nature. It's a much deeper dive than just scratching the surface like we're used to, but *so* worth the trip. At this level we can understand why we're experiencing symptoms and, perhaps more importantly, how we can naturally move back into balance, a balance that doesn't fall somewhere *on* the chart acceptable but "*off* the chart" amazing!

SO, KEEP IN MIND

This book isn't designed to help you lose weight. You may find, however, that it helps you to identify what you've been craving.

It isn't designed to heal disease. You may find, however, that it brings to you simple practices where you will see physical and emotional improvement in your body and mind.

It isn't designed to win you new friends. You may find, however, a new perspective on the people already in your life. You may find ways to improve strained relationships, and perhaps learn to forgive. And as for new relationships to follow, you'll see the necessity of getting out of your own way.

This book isn't about making your job better. It may, however, give you the impetus to reach for new heights and to discover that you're so much more than you think and that you're able to unveil your true self and your life's purpose.

Wellness Archetype Quiz

On the following pages, you will find 20 paired statements. Choose the statement in each pair that best fits your personality. If neither statement in a pairing sounds like it fits who you are, choose the one that you feel fits best.

As your personality guides you through your choices of the following statements, you'll ultimately discover what Wellness Archetype you identify with the most: The Visionary, The Artist, The Transformer, The Pacifist, or The Rock. Each archetype is associated with a natural element: Space, Air, Fire, Water and Earth. The inherent qualities of the Wellness Archetype and corresponding natural element(s) you identify with the most showcase themselves in your own physical and emotional qualities.[49]

As you read the following chapters, you'll see what they – and you – look like in balance, and yet how they can morph and manifest themselves in you when they're out of balance.

We have all the Elements in us, to varying degrees – that's what joins us all together collectively yet distinguishes each of us as unique. It's the Element(s) you gravitate towards the most that you can identify as your life's "blueprint."

So, let's get started by finding out what your personality reveals!

- **A.** I see the wisdom in letting someone talk through a problem themselves rather than rushing in to give them advice.
- **C.** I'm very results-oriented, and I like to solve problems.

- **A.** On more than one occasion when I have been stopped at a traffic light people have blown their horn at me because I was distracted with something else and didn't notice the light had turned green.
- **E.** I try to give my undivided attention to whatever task I'm performing so I'm not easily distracted.

- **C.** I lean more toward making quick decisions based entirely on the facts.
- **D.** Whenever I take a stand, it's usually after careful consideration of the interests of everyone involved.

- **D.** I often feel like my efforts go unnoticed.
- **E.** I really don't like being in the spotlight.

- **C.** When I'm put under stress, my first reaction is anger.
- **B.** When I'm confronted with a stressful situation, my first reaction is panic.

- **B.** I get bored very quickly.
- **E.** I can spend hours concentrating on one thing.

- **A.** When working through a project I can easily get carried away with other ideas and lose focus.
- **C.** I get great satisfaction checking off as "completed" items on a to-do list.

B. Unexpected change can send me into a tailspin.
A. When new circumstances present themselves, rather than resisting the change my first reaction is how can I accommodate it into the present situation.

A. I can "dream big" but I find it difficult to convert my ideas into practicality.
D. If you show me how to manage something, I'll keep it running smoothly.

B. Too many ideas sometimes overwhelm me.
A. The more ideas and options, the better.

A. I have a tendency to leave things scattered around my work area or my home.
E. I'm very methodical as I complete tasks.

B. It doesn't bother me if my friends disagree. Everyone is entitled to their own point of view.
D. I believe I would be a really good mediator because I enjoy bringing people with opposing views to a common ground.

C. I can come across as judgmental.
D. I generally give people the benefit of the doubt.

C. I have high expectations of myself and others.
E. I don't like to be the leader.

D. I go out of my way to avoid confrontations.
E. I prefer to maintain the status quo.

- **C.** I feel best when I have pre-planned for every possible scenario.
- **B.** I'm not big into pre-planning a lot of details in projects. I figure I can wing it as I go.

- **E.** I have one or two close friends I prefer hanging out with.
- **D.** I have a strong community of friends.

- **D.** I would describe my voice as soothing.
- **B.** I have a tendency to speak quickly.

- **E.** I prefer to read a detailed news story in depth.
- **A.** I prefer to just hear the highlights.

- **B.** I am prone to impulse spending.
- **C.** I wisely calculate my expenditures.

RESULTS

A. _____ **THE VISIONARY** - *SPACE*

B. _____ **THE ARTIST** - *AIR*

C. _____ **THE TRANSFORMER** - *FIRE*

D. _____ **THE PACIFIST** - *WATER*

E. _____ **THE ROCK** - *EARTH*

WHAT TO DO WITH THE RESULTS

After you have finished your selections, count up the number of times you chose each letter, A through E, and write that number next to the corresponding archetype. The archetype that has the highest number for you is the Wellness Archetype and corresponding natural element you associate with most closely.

The following chapters describe each of these Wellness Archetypes in depth. They discuss physically and emotionally what each archetype looks like in balance, and out of balance. When you see what they look like in balance and out of balance, you'll be able to gauge where you are on the scale of physical and emotional well-being. If you're feeling out of balance, there's advice and methods on how to get yourself back on track and realigned with the best parts of your nature.

For many of you, your results may be high in one specific archetype. For others, your results may reflect an affinity towards multiple archetypes. If you find that you gravitate to multiple Wellness Archetypes, feel free to go through each of those following chapters and implement what resonates with you.

When you know what archetype and element you identify with the most you have a more personalized road map to vibrant health.

The Visionary

DOES THE VISIONARY SOUND LIKE YOU?

When others may think they're stuck in their circumstances with no way out, it's always the Visionary who sees things more expansively. They look through a different kind of lens. It's more than just designing an "escape hatch." It's a lens that actually bends the circumstances away from challenging towards opportunistic. It's someone who sees well beyond the immediacy of what is in front of them. It's someone who can envision potential and sees limitless possibilities.

ATTRIBUTES:
- Are you open-minded?
- Are you effortlessly accommodating to others?
- Are you boundless in your vision?
- Do you accept your own and others' situations without judgment?
- Do you see the latent qualities or opportunities for good and growth in your circumstances, even when they're challenging?

YET, PERHAPS:
- Do you find it hard to focus on one idea at a time?
- Do you have difficulty anchoring your thoughts?
- Does tending to details drive you crazy?

If you answered "yes" to most of these questions, then you naturally align most closely with the Space Element. You want to foster your visionary nature, but keep it balanced as well. Dream big and continue to envision possibilities and opportunities, as you are inclined to do, but keep your feet planted firmly on the earth. Keeping your Visionary nature balanced will certainly take some necessary grounding, clearing and nourishing.

A REAL-LIFE VISIONARY

After 25 years of working out, Diane is still the best personal trainer I've ever known. As a young attorney putting in long hours, I began to see the toll a sedentary lifestyle could take. It was then I decided getting in tip-top physical shape was going to be my new project. Joining a gym and going to fitness classes wasn't what I had in mind. Instead, I was in search of a personal trainer; someone who would design work out programs just for me, provide individualized attention, and put me on the fast track to where I wanted to be. In short, I was looking to hire a drill sergeant of sorts. My mother often spoke about a physical therapist who worked in her chiropractor's office and suggested that she may be the trainer I was looking for. Although my mother always spoke very highly of Diane, I was a bit skeptical. After all, if she didn't work in a gym, then how could she fill the bill of the hard-core drill sergeant I was in the market for? My question was unequivocally answered at our first meeting.

It certainly wasn't a drill sergeant attitude that Diane exuded, it was the example she set. She was friendly, knowledgeable, fit and confident. As I found out through our conversation, she had worked as a personal trainer for over 25 years. She had owned, and recently sold, one of the most successful fitness studios in Pittsburgh and had trained professional as well as amateur athletes. But, more than her resume, she was her own walking and talking advertisement for what "tip-top physical condition" looked like. Seems it wasn't a drill sergeant I was looking for; it was a role model.

We talked about my fitness goals and she evaluated me for strength, flexibility and cardio capacity. After our second meeting, I left armed with a rather modest arsenal: a step with risers, an exercise band, and a cassette tape with workout music on it, along with a few routines she designed specifically for me. I supplied the free weights (and the necessary commitment) and before long I had a workout schedule, "stepping" to the hottest music at that time like Blondie and INXS. Over a short amount of time my devotion paid off as I was in the best physical shape of my life.

A short time later, Diane opened her own fitness studio down the hall from the chiropractor; this one much smaller than the one she recently sold. I excitedly became a member of her studio, along with a slew of others she already knew personally – current and former clients, friends and family of clients, and chiropractic patients. It always amazed me the wide range of people Diane attracted, and she catered to each one of us like we were her only client. Men, women, and children, well-to-do professionals and entrepreneurs alike, all with varied physical shapes and sizes. Our eclectic group instantly bonded with each other. The reason? It was the space that Diane created, the feeling that permeated the studio. If you knew Diane, then you knew her "family." You were part of the "fold," the fan base. She made everyone feel special, welcomed, and appreciated. We happily shared our time with her and with one another. Working out and getting in shape actually became an added bonus.

Looking back now, I can't remember exactly why I left Diane's – probably to pursue yoga full time or something like that – but I caught up with her several years later. She still owned her own fitness studio, but she had moved a short distance away to another building. I remember thinking when I first walked up the stairs to her second-floor studio that this physical space had some very strange nuances to it and was definitely more awkwardly shaped than her previous fitness studio.

Upon arriving after climbing two flights of stairs, you turned an immediate right and walked through a doorway directly toward a desk with two chairs out front where she greeted you, if she (or her staff, now) wasn't busy tending to other clients. It was also at her desk that she measured you, every 10 weeks, to ensure you lost weight and/or built muscle where you needed to. After she logged the progress of your measurements on your client card, she custom designed a workout to get you to the next level of fitness and physical transformation.

To the left of the desk was a larger area where free weights, exercise bands and weightlifting gloves were stowed and where a modest, yet adequate, array of equipment was set up. Off that room was a long, narrow room enclosed with interior and exterior windows on each side, one wall of windows looked into the equipment room and along the opposite long wall was a row of windows looking outside and down into the parking lot. Hardly a usable space by anyone else's judgment, but then again, Diane didn't have just anyone else's judgment.

She declared it her "cardio room" and very meticulously lined up treadmills, ellipticals, and stationary bikes at an angle to accommodate the physical logistics of the room, all facing the wall of windows looking outside. A neat accommodation for sure, but it didn't end there. She proceeded to line up BOSUs balls (those blue half-balls) along the wall of windows which faced into the equipment room. It was this set-up that became her "signature workout," a program she exclusively designed as an hour-long cardio/body sculpting workout where we did some stepping up and down on the BOSUs mixed in with some body sculpting moves for 5 minutes. Then at designated times throughout the hour, we stepped off the BOSUs and jumped on a cardio machine of our choice for another 3 minutes solid and then it was back on the BOSUs for more stepping and sculpting. Not only was the program an instant success with her clients, but Diane went on to ultimately trademark the name of that workout. An amazing development for a program that was originally inspired to merely accommodate an oddly shaped space.

There was also a room to the right of Diane's desk that she originally rented out to one of her friend-clients who sold workout clothes. It seemed like a perfect match; selling workouts, and workout apparel; and it was for a while. Then her friend moved and when she left so did her racks of inventory as well as her steady monetary contribution to Diane's rent. To anyone else, they faced a dried-up stream of income as well as a literal empty space.

Once again, we watched as Diane's visionary astuteness went to work. Rather than try to look for another tenant to fill that space, Diane re-designed it to hold her "abs classes" as she scattered BOSUs randomly across the carpeted floor. Two times each hour, for whomever was in the studio working out at the time, they stopped what they were doing, entered the newly designed space, and "did abs" for about 20 minutes under her direction. Looking back now, you just couldn't imagine the space being any other way.

It wasn't just envisioning physical space that was Diane's forté, it was envisioning ideas. It was seeing otherwise mundane, concrete things and recognizing their potential. Over her many years as a fitness instructor, you can only imagine the number of body measurements she recorded of her clients—concrete evidence of how fast and how much they lost fat and built muscle under her masterful direction. She saw these measurements, however, as more than just numbers; she saw them as patterns – as guides, if you will – and as possibilities. Possibilities to show others just how their bodies could change over time, if they could only see themselves in the future. She envisioned a brand new business tool for weight loss: a program that took your present photo image and transformed it showing what your image would look like at various stages of weight loss with new measurements after adopting various fitness routines. It was this tool that she later patented into an amazingly successful business venture that has caught the eyes, ears and interest of some heavy hitters in the weight loss industry.

The lasting impression I have of Diane is her wonderful gift to take whatever she has and envision it to its fullest potential. Whether it's transforming physical space or developing cutting-edge ideas, undoubtedly the most profound gift that she has is envisioning the potential in her clients.

MORE ABOUT THE SPACE ELEMENT

On the most subtle level, Space works "behind the scenes." It is the field which hosts form, creation and flow. Space is the still, blank canvas upon which our thoughts and emotions are drawn. It is the canvas upon which we paint our ideas, our dreams, and our life. It is a welcoming host to whatever it contains or dances upon it. Remember, we can paint any kind of picture we want to on this canvas. Simply put, the Space Element embodies and holds all potential.

SPACE AS VAST

When someone says the word "Space" we may immediately think of that luxurious blanket of blackness, bejeweled with twinkling stars, earth's vast canopy we call "outer space," the cosmos, or the heavens. Or perhaps we call to mind the panorama of a beautiful, clear, bright blue sky that stretches out before us with no discernible beginning or end. Whatever the image, Space's essence is "the unoccupied."

SPACE AS EMPTY

You may have glanced through those photo galleries of abandoned amusement parks which often appear on the internet. Those images conjure up an almost palpable feeling of emptiness as you sense the stark contrast. Space between the vibrantly animated teems of people who once strolled their meandering concrete walks; guests who once filled those parks to the brim with their joyous laughter and screams of excitement, contrasted now with the emptiness, devoid of life that pervades their grounds. It's only the vacancy we now feel. A perfect example of an unseen "host" that resides in the background, as the background, into which existence once took form.

SPACE AS GAPS BETWEEN OUR BREATH AND OUR WORDS

Think of space as the distance or gap between things. Think about the brief pauses between your breath cycles; those infinitesimal yet pivotal moments which allow the flow of your breath to change direction without you even thinking about it or exerting any effort —so necessary for you to survive. Think about the brief gaps between the words you speak every day all day long—those spaces or pauses so necessary for you to effectively communicate with others without jumbling your words together lest you have anincomprehensiblestreamofconsciousness. (An incomprehensible stream of consciousness).

SPACE AS GAPS BETWEEN THOUGHTS

Think about the undetectable yet crucial breaks between the constant bombardment of your thoughts all day long – so necessary to allow them to come into form, be sorted through, and either be discarded or to blossom.

SPACE TO ALLOW US TO GROW

Space provides the room to allow things to necessarily come into form, to change and to grow. Think about an embryo and the womb in which it develops. The space in which it is brought into existence, hosted, nourished and in which it grows.

SPACE AS STORAGE

It's a natural inclination for our mind to conjure up ideas of how to fill up space. From our egos' perspective, filling up space boasts of productivity; even cleverness. After all, what good is space that is not filled with something? When we're shopping for a new home or apartment our eyes light up when we see extra space to hold our belongings and store our stuff. "Here's how I designed this space," we might say. Or: "I thought here would be a perfect space to put this." Or: "I'm not sure what to do with this space yet."

We treat idle time the same as we feel compelled to fill it up with busy-work, or activities to focus our attention so we don't leave anything empty in our lives. We focus on this or that; something useful or not. Either way, we view space as just begging us to do something with it.

SPACE IN OUR BODY

Let's focus on our own body now and contemplate the various spaces it holds within. Think of our lungs as spaces which swell with the air we inhale; the twisting tube of our digestive tract through which the food we ingest passes; the emptiness of an unfilled bladder; and the delicate spaces that exist between each vertebra and each rib. Think about the even smaller vessels like our arteries, veins, lymph channels, and urinary tract designed to accommodate the flow of fluids; or the multitude of nerves throughout our body which function as pathways through which impulses are carried.

When we consider the more concrete examples of space inside our body, we see how necessary it is to keep those spaces intact and to maintain their integrity – no more and no less – otherwise, our entire form and function will collapse.

The spaces within our body must remain clear and unobstructed so our body can properly operate; so, we can breathe fully; so, we can digest and assimilate completely; and so, our blood can circulate freely throughout the body.

When space in the body increases it necessarily decreases the integrity of our tissue structure. For example, an increase in the space within our bones could result in conditions like osteoporosis – more space, less bone. Similarly, the destruction of nerve cells in the body could result in conditions like Parkinson's disease – a decrease in nerve cells in the brain which are responsible for movement. A decrease in these neurons creates gaps (or spaces) which disrupt the flow of communication that once existed – more space, less cellular messaging.

When space in the body decreases it could mean a collapse of the form, like a collapsed lung or a pinched nerve. In each case, the integrity of the space is encroached upon and lessened. Decreased space in the body could also mean that unwanted mass is taking up residence in a certain place, like a clogged artery, for example. An increase in the fatty deposits of cholesterol, which take up space in a normally formed artery, compromise optimal blood flow, and can lead to heart disease. Likewise, formation of a growth or tumor in the body crowds out space and blocks free flowing blood, prevents proper organ functioning, or interrupts a system process, which can also lead to disease.

SPACE IN OUR MIND

The integrity of our mind space, just like the integrity of any other space, must be maintained; no more and no less.

When we refer to Space increasing in the mind, think of losing focus as your mind turns away from your tasks at hand. You begin to "zone out," or turn numb. You look, but you're not seeing. You hear, but you're not listening. You can't account for your thoughts as they drift away or evaporate altogether. Remember, Space is formless. So, the more Space that continues to expand in your mind without being contained, the less form will reside there – thoughts, ideas, emotions, feelings, and boundaries become less structured and begin to morph into one another. There is indeed a destruction of form.

Often if your mind space is not adequately contained, you may find yourself floating away "in thought" without a firm anchor to ground you. The image comes to mind of an astronaut floating in space connected to the station with only a safety tether. But for that safety tether, the astronaut would just float away.

When we refer to Space decreasing in the mind, that's when our mind is filled with clutter, which can take the form of extraneous thoughts, usually thoughts of things that already happened, or things that never will happen. This kind of clutter prohibits us from thinking clearly or moving forward. It takes up the space of original ideas, ingenious plans, and creative connections. Our mind space becomes "crowded" and unavailable to host healthy thoughts and emotions.

In fact, just think of all that space we've carved out and designated in our minds where we pile up old encounters and hurt feelings. These are spaces where we neatly stack away imagined conversations and scarring arguments, hypothetical speeches, judgements, grudges and drawn conclusions – which we can deftly and unfailingly call to mind not only with the slightest trigger, but with the efficiency as if they were stored away using the Dewey Decimal system.

When our mind is grounded and undisturbed, however, we are able to totally absorb the present moment and experience the true essence of the Space Element: quiet, still, subtle and peaceful.

THE ACTION PLAN FOR THE VISIONARY

Keep envisioning "the big picture," but make sure to create boundaries to contain and maintain your mind space so it doesn't expand too much. You don't want to become carried away and lose focus.

While your quality of effortlessly accepting new situations and people is a virtue, you must have some sense of clarity to discern and define what is beneficial and what is detrimental to you.

You want to keep a clear mind to host your unlimited wellspring of ideas. As a host and a vessel for ideas, your mind space is a place that could easily accumulate unwanted or irrelevant clutter. You want to keep it clean and orderly.

You want to foster your internal terrain (your mind space) where healthy thoughts and ideas for you and for others can be planted and have room to grow and develop. Since Space is the host to your ideas and intentions, you want to nourish that environment.

TECHNIQUES FOR BRINGING THE VISIONARY BACK INTO BALANCE

THINKING: The mind is the space into which thoughts and emotions are born. If your mind is cluttered, your thoughts and emotions will follow suit.

Imagine if you were invited to a friend's house for dinner. You arrived to find no one home. A few minutes later your host arrived profusely apologizing and obviously all out of sorts. He escorts you inside and you find his home in total disarray. There is no place for you to sit—but it's just as well because he hasn't invited you to do so anyway. He flings open the refrigerator and finds some leftovers. He throws them into a pot and slams it on the stove as he turns the heat up to high. Then he proceeds to re-hash to you an upsetting conversation he had earlier with his ex-wife. How can that be a pleasant experience for you as a guest? There is clearly no room for you there; neither physically, nor emotionally. You'd want to high-tail it out of there as fast as you could! It works the same with the space in your own mind.

Clutter will wreak havoc with the Visionary. Your mind space will, in effect, decrease as it becomes populated with extraneous content. There is no room for new thoughts and emotions to enter, take hold and grow. Clearing your mind invites mental debris to settle. It makes space and allows you to welcome new thoughts and emotions to conceptualize and thrive.

That being said, however, you don't want the space in your mind to unnecessarily increase either. While "thinking big" is undoubtedly one of the Visionary's most noble traits, with it comes the danger of inflating too much if not properly contained. Your expansiveness can turn into "spaciness" as you can become unfocused and tend to veer off into irrelevant content.

Containing your mental space is integral to staying tethered to reality. Learning how to rein in your expansive nature is a task worth pursuing.

MEDITATION: The easiest and most effective way for you, the Visionary, to maintain the integrity and clarity of your mental space, improve your focus and strengthen concentration is through meditation. It's like tilling good, healthy soil so that healthy crops (ideas) may be planted, nourished, and grow.

We don't realize how much time we spend analyzing the past or anticipating the future. While we think we're being productive in all this "analysis," it's actually producing clutter in our mind. We have so much "background noise" going on in our head, we can't focus on much of anything. When the mind is clear, however, you can give your full attention to whatever crosses your path, with the proper focus and flexibility necessary for you to act. A clear mind can see all the options and all the resources available to it. Meditation brings us clarity and focus. It helps to anchor our thoughts while also making room to see even more possibilities. The integrity of our mind space is maintained: It is neither drastically increased, nor decreased.

You can begin meditating right now. The best way to begin meditating is to sit, either cross-legged on the floor, or upright in a chair; shoulders down and away from your ears; eyes closed; mouth relaxed and chin slightly tucked in. Let go of thoughts or circumstances you've been struggling with, outside noises, or other distractions. Just let them pass right through you. Begin by focusing on different parts of your physical body or focus on a positive thought, or an uplifting message. We tend to complicate the process. Keep it simple. Dr. Robert Svoboda, one of the most talented Ayurvedic practitioners in the United States, assures that "Anything can be a meditation, as long as it is sincere and heartfelt."[2]

If you're not sure you're doing it "right," there are many meditation apps to choose from, but downloading them isn't enough. Make sure to carve out time in your schedule every day to meditate (morning, afternoon or evening), even if it's just for a few minutes. It is never time wasted, but don't expect miracles overnight. That's not how it works.

Over time you'll begin to notice a subtle but profound change in yourself. You'll find that your concentration will gradually improve, mental clutter will dissipate, your thoughts will more readily anchor themselves and take shape, and you will cultivate that much-needed mind space, all of which is integral to balancing the Visionary.

JOURNALING: This is a process that is almost custom-made for the Visionary. Ground your ideas by writing them down. Create an action plan; make lists; provide details. The Visionary tends to keep things "in their head." Journaling is actually the process which transforms those ideas into readable concepts. Pouring out your ideas onto paper frees up the space in your mind to plan out how to execute them. Journaling also promotes mental clarity as it allows you to process emotions and gain insights.[3]

Keep tapping into your mind and let the ideas pour out. The goal is to maintain the integrity of your mind-space. It's a manual form of data dumping, and a necessary way to process that data. It allows you to make connections between your ideas, your thoughts and your emotions. Journaling also helps you to learn more about yourself, how to make room for your ideas, how to foster your thoughts and improve their chances of succeeding.

DECLUTTER YOUR HOME, YOUR OFFICE AND YOUR CAR TO CREATE ORDERLY, CLEAN SPACES IN WHICH TO LIVE, WORK AND TRAVEL: We don't even notice how a cluttered physical environment contributes to a cluttered mental environment. "A place for everything and everything in its place," as the saying goes. Tidiness allows us the space to breathe, both literally and figuratively.

I remember seeing a cartoon of a woman sitting at a desk talking over her shoulder to a male coworker who was standing behind her chair.

They were staring at the piles of papers stacked up on both sides of the desk towering over the woman's head. Her message to her colleague read: "We need a new piling system."

I used to work for an attorney whose office looked like the one in that cartoon. It was so cluttered, the piles of paper were literally falling in on each other. When you opened his office door to enter you had to gingerly walk across the floor with the same antics and dexterity as if you were walking across a minefield; lest you kick over one of the paper piles. It's not like you were trying to make it to one of the two chairs in front of his desk because there was no room to sit on either one. Both seats held heavy stacks of papers as well. I often took a seat on the arm of the chair closest to the door (I'm sure I had to move something to uncover that space as well). He had the air vents blocked with paper stacks. He also had artifacts of past trials strewn throughout his office which ranged from exhibit boards illustrating a forged signature in a contract dispute to old engine parts he offered as evidence in a product liability case. You would think that mess would indicate industriousness and a "nose to the grindstone" work ethic. Not really. Every day you would likely find Frank lingering in the downstairs restaurant of our office building reading the newspaper or "holding court" with his cronies for a good part of the morning and throughout the day. It shouldn't come as a shock to know that it wasn't just his office that was in disarray. It was his entire life.

Don't let your physical or mental space look like Frank's office. Clearing your physical space will automatically help to clear your mental space. You'll be surprised how your ideas will grow and become realized when you give them the space in which to enter.

FEELING: Another effective way to balance the Space Element is to literally get in touch with the Earth Element. Physically spending time in nature or even touching the ground will help stabilize the Visionary and provide them with a more anchored perspective and experience. It is important that you re-establish and strengthen your foundation on the earth.

SPEND TIME OUTDOORS: Immerse yourself in the beauty of nature. Walking, hiking, or a leisurely bike ride are excellent ways to ground yourself in nature and to interact with your physical environment.

TRY "EARTHING": Perhaps Thoreau put it best when he said: "As for the complex ways of living, I love them not, however much I practice them. In as many places as possible, I will get my feet down to the earth."[4]

Establishing a literal connection to the earth goes a long way in grounding the Visionary. The earth carries an energy that nourishes our own energetic body and by making physical contact with the earth, our body receives an immediate charge of that energy. We mostly live and work indoors and when we do go outside, our shoes prevent us from directly connecting with the earth.[5]

"Earthing" is walking barefoot on soil, grass or sand. While it promises many physical benefits like decreased levels of pain and inflammation, reduced stress levels, and even improved circulation, the Visionary will particularly notice a grounding to their thoughts.

HANDLING EARTH: Gardening, working with clay, or even holding a stone will impart much needed calming and channeling to the Visionary.

To balance the energy in their head, it does the Visionary good to remember that the world under the earth's surface is teeming with multitudes of microcosms. Gardening provides the perfect vantage point for you to see with different eyes. Sinking your hands in the soil will ground you whether you're growing a backyard garden or planting herbs in windowsill pots.

But what if you have no time to garden? An easy option may be to buy some children's natural clay, or simply pick up a small rock or stone. Just the act of forming the clay or holding the rock or stone in your hands, while visualizing your feet planted firmly on the earth, will help channel your big ideas into something more "real." The act of literally handling a natural element will help to ground your body and your mind.

EATING: Cheese puffs, popcorn, puffed cereals and airy breads – they all have increased space and decreased mass. Keep in mind that the qualities of the foods you consume create those same qualities in your body.

ROOTED FOODS: The Visionary will especially benefit by incorporating root vegetables into their diet. Root vegetables have a dense structure and because they grow underground they absorb a tremendous amount of nutrients from the soil.

The Visionary in particular wants to draw the energy that's in their head downward into their body in order to ground themselves. The directional growth of root vegetables, downward into the earth, is exceptionally effective in balancing the upward, outward, and naturally expansive qualities of the Space Element. Root vegetables are a wonderful addition to your diet as you work to remain rooted and grounded on the earth.

Root vegetables have a special affinity for our lower body. The root vegetables which grow downwards and outwards like rutabagas, beets, sweet potatoes, and fennel will be relaxing and unwinding for you. Root vegetables which grow downward and inward (those that have a long, tapered root) like carrots, daikon radish, and parsnips will provide you with a sense of presence and awareness.[6]

Root vegetables will create feelings of grounding and stability, reining in your tendency to expand just enough to bring you back into balance.

FAVOR COOKED FOOD OVER RAW: You should also emphasize cooked food over raw food for a couple of reasons. Food that is cooked is generally easier to digest and assimilate than food that is consumed raw. Raw foods require us to expend more metabolic energy in order to digest them. Cooking does a lot of the digestive work for us by breaking down food more completely than we ever could if we consumed it in its raw state. In fact, cooking actually performs the role of pre-digesting the food before you even eat it so the burden on your digestive system to perform that work is greatly lessened. It makes more nutrients readily available to us.[7]

Raw foods are energetically light in nature, an energy that you, the Visionary, must try to avoid. Remember, the Visionary's natural tendency is to expand and become carried away. Eating food that is energetically "light" will only carry you further out of balance. You need to be grounded, not floating away. Think back to the astronaut floating in space connected to the safety tether. To achieve balance, the Visionary does best by consuming food that is energetically grounding. Consuming cooked foods increases the Earth and Water Elements in the body, both of which have a heavier essence which will help you to regain your balance.

STAY NOURISHED: Going back to the fundamental guidance for the Space Element: Maintain its integrity, don't let it increase too much and don't let it decrease too much. Skipping meals will increase the emptiness in your stomach. The less you eat, the more space is created. Your body is used to being fed. Deliberately leaving it empty will disrupt your body's natural rhythms and systems and will particularly wreak havoc with your digestive fire.

Nourish that space in your body. Feed it at regular intervals to cultivate a feeling of satisfaction. High quality, whole foods (preferably organic) will provide the nutrients to satisfy your body (and your mind). Your organs will be fed and satisfied so that you won't have a tendency to reach for other unhealthy food to "fill you up".

By the same token, don't crowd out the space by overeating. Be aware of what and how much you're consuming. Just as we don't want to fill free time with busy activities that are meaningless to us, we don't want to fill our stomach just to feel full. Think about "nourishing" the empty space rather than just "filling it up."

The Artist

DOES THE ARTIST SOUND LIKE YOU?

It's almost impossible to stop the Artist from creating. It's what they were born to do. Their creative canvas could be a white page, a block of wood, a lump of clay, a blank Word-document screen, or an empty staff. Their instrument could be a paintbrush, a wood carving knife, their bare hands, words, or musical notes. Regardless of the medium, the Artist brings form, texture, and tone to life as they communicate and transmit their thoughts and feelings into the world.

ATTRIBUTES:
- Are you always involved with a project or activity?
- Are you fueled by inspiration and creativity?
- Are you social by nature?
- Do you freely articulate your feelings?
- Do you have a wide range of interests?

YET, PERHAPS:
- Do you tend to take on too many activities at once?
- Do you have a tendency to burn out rather quickly?
- Can you become anxious and overwhelmed by what you've taken on?

If you answered "yes" to most of these questions, then you naturally align most closely with the Air Element. You want to encourage your artistic nature, but keep it balanced as well. Keeping the Artist's creative stream manageable, yet free flowing, is the crucial point of balance. We want to help control the influx but provide a means of unobstructed yet measured release. Providing direction and structure to that released flow will help to channel it into organization.

A REAL-LIFE ARTIST

Don (or "Uncle Don" as I have always called him) is a very dear man and close family friend. I've known him and his family all my life. After a career in education (he was a high school English teacher and guidance counselor) he retired several years ago. I don't know that he ever experienced a void left by his former job because he had so many other on-going activities on the sidelines waiting for his meticulous care and attention.

Whether he calls himself a "woodworker" or a "carpenter," his passion has always been working with his hands. He built a stunning library in his own home and one of even surpassed beauty in his daughter's Victorian home. He has whittled away stylish shillelaghs which he loves to give away as gifts; and has even tried his hand at making stained glass windows. I'm not sure if he missed his professional calling or not, but Uncle Don's perfectionist nature and attention to detail certainly lend themselves to a successful craftsman.

He knows wood like the back of his hand. He knows how it smells, how it breathes, how it reacts to heat and cold and, most importantly, how it carves. Ever the teacher, he taught me how to spot a Shag Bark Hickory tree – its bark flairs out from the trunk like those trees you see in cartoon forests.

The first time I witnessed his woodworking genius from beginning to end was when he built a doghouse for my Labrador Retriever, Tasha. Calling this structure, a "doghouse" relegated it to a category far below its stature. Actually, it was more like a Swiss Chalet; minus the snow and absent the skiers. Although, if you closed your eyes and really listened hard, you could almost confuse an occasional howl from its four-legged resident as "yodeling."

Tasha's house had blueprints. My parents' house didn't even have blueprints. In fact, no one I had ever known to that point had blueprints. Her house had a vaulted ceiling with exposed wooden beams. If she had ever entertained guests, they would have been duly impressed. I remember my dad discreetly raising his eyebrows when Uncle Don presented him the list of materials he needed for construction: the numerous 2x4's for the main structure, one 1x4 for trim around the front door (not like there was a back door), plywood for the floor and genuine cedar shakes for the exterior. Its grandeur (as far as doghouses have grandeur) was summed up by my dad's clever nickname for Tasha's new abode: the "Tash Mahal." It was indeed a work of art – and Tasha, who ultimately had the final word, was thrilled with her new digs.

In the summer of 2014, Uncle Don lent his artistry to my own home as he recruited my dad to help him transform a double door closet in my upstairs loft into a stunning floor to ceiling book case; replete with mahogany stained, lacquered cubicles that were enclosed behind two French doors with elegantly curved handles. He placed tape lights along the inside perimeter. As I watched my bookcase come into being, it was clear Uncle Don could easily get lost in his work; pencil clenched between his lips, as he contemplated 1/4's of inches.

That was the same summer he decided to write limericks, which would become one of his newly acquired past times, albeit a very short one, and for good reason. Uncle Don started writing limericks about family members and friends. He wrote one about my dad, and one about me (which I don't really remember other than the word "Italian" was in it). As he felt he was improving in his "art," he extended his purview to acquaintances who were friendly enough to reveal just a little bit about themselves; just enough to give the limerick some humorous substance. It seemed like he was on quite a roll until he got an icy reception from a woman in his bowling league. It wasn't anything offensive that he wrote (her husband actually took it with a laugh), but she was quite put off after realizing that Uncle Don uninvitedly took the liberty of commenting upon her behavior and putting his observations into a rhyme (a limerick) without her consent and which she apparently didn't think was so cute.

To say Uncle Don is social is an understatement. He loves being around people, striking up a conversation to see if they fish, bowl, or know anything about woodworking. He's still a member of his bowling league (although he avoids the woman he wrote the limerick about), and he loves to host bluegill fish-frys.

For the last year or so I've been helping him out with his diet. Uncle Don is a picky eater with a pretty variable appetite. He does, however, have an insatiable sweet tooth. He confessed to me, with a twinkle in his eye, that he eats blueberry pie for breakfast. He also tried to get one over on his daughter and me when he attempted to convince us he needed to eat Reese's peanut butter cups for the "protein." Ah huh.

Uncle Don loves to tell stories, especially fishing stories. He also loves to tell the story of when he took me and my dad fishing. My dad and I were a captive audience, and Uncle Don relished being the instructor. We went fishing for bluegills and rowed out to the middle of Virgin Lake, one of Uncle Don's favorite fishing spots. After we reeled in our catch for the day, he instructed my dad to row us back to shore. My dad said for some reason it was very difficult to row us back. We finally reached the shore, but my dad just couldn't explain why he felt so tuckered out. Rowing out onto the lake was much easier. When we reached shore, Uncle Don realized that he neglected pull up the anchor and unknowingly made my dad row us back dragging the anchor. Oh, Uncle Don got a big chuckle out of that one—and many miles out of that story!

Uncle Don seamlessly moves from one interest to the next. He plays the harmonica, and he loves to sing. Whenever he comes over to visit, he makes himself right at home as he takes a seat at the piano and begins to play. The last I talked with him he was in the midst of writing his own memoir about his fishing adventures. He wrote out his autobiography in long hand and recruited a member of his bowling league to type it up on her computer. He loves history and, for a time, served as the church historian.

All told, Uncle Don is the consummate artist. He has a creative streak and displays it throughout his varied interests and on-going projects.

MORE ABOUT THE AIR ELEMENT

Air is the necessary elemental force that breathes life into our physical movement. If Space is the host to our thoughts, feelings and emotions, then the Air Element provides the propulsive force to sweep them from the vessel of our mind into reality. It provides the force for our physical body to move and for our ideas to be born.

AIR AS MOVEMENT

When we think of air the image that usually comes to mind is that of wind. We can only see and feel the evidence of its movement, but we've all enjoyed a breeze blowing softly across our face. We've all been surprised to watch a gust of wind suddenly pick up a pile of leaves and hurriedly usher them across the yard in mad swirl, and we've all likely squinted our eyes and shivered as we've forged through a blustery snowstorm.

AIR AS FLOW AND PROPULSION

Old-fashioned windmills used the force generated by the Air Element to create rotational energy by means of its blades or "sails." Originally, that wind energy was primarily used for pumping water and grinding grain.

While wind power technology has greatly advanced, the basic concept still goes back to the force of the Air Element. It is the flow of the air – the wind that it creates – which turns propellers around a rotor. The rotor is connected to a main shaft which spins a generator to create electricity.

AIR AS TRANSMISSION AND COMMUNICATION

When we speak, we send pressurized air across our vocal cords, through the larynx, and out through our mouth cavity. The loudness of our voice is controlled by the force with which we expel the air. Keep in mind it is air which fuels our entire verbal communication system. When we speak, it's always on the exhalation of air as it flows across our vocal cords.[8]

Sound is actually the energy produced when something vibrates. The vibration of the object forces the air around it to vibrate as well. As the air vibrates it carries that energy out from the source in all directions. Eventually the air inside our ears starts to vibrate. And that's when we begin to perceive that energy as sound. What we hear are sound waves produced by the vibrations of air molecules. Air is responsible for the recording and the transmission.[9]

AIR AS FORCE OR BLOCKAGE

On the climate stage we see the continuous influence of air on our weather patterns. High pressure systems, which are a whirling mass of cool, dry air, generally bring with them fair weather, light winds and sunny skies. Low pressure systems, however, are a whirling mass of warm, moist air, and generally bring with them cloudy, rainy or snowy weather. We've also seen how huge pockets of air can simply sit over a geographical region and completely block the flow of other weather systems moving in.

AIR IN DISARRAY

Perhaps you've endured turbulence in an airplane. It's no doubt an uneasy feeling for most of us and likely the closest we ever want to get to experiencing the sheer force of the Air Element.

People who live in parts of Texas, South Dakota, Oklahoma, Nebraska, and Kansas, or "Tornado Alley," as it's known, can certainly speak first-hand about just how fierce and destructive the Air Element can become. When the terrain is flat, those swirling vortexes of destruction can pick up tremendous speed and intensity and can turn into an unbelievable force to be reckoned with as they destroy everything in their path.

Hurricane force winds showcase yet another destructive force and form the Air Element can take. It's hard to imagine it is the same Air Element that lightly brushes across our cheek as a summer breeze which can drastically transform in its speed, power and intensity when the conditions change.

AIR IN OUR BODY

Our breath is likely the first thing that comes to mind when we think of the Air Element in our body. It's seemingly inconsequential qualities of lightness and mobility render it almost undetectable. But our breath isn't the only evidence of Air's effect in our body. In fact, its sheer force is responsible for all the movement and processes that we experience.

Consider the intricate network of transmitting messages between nerve cells. According to Ayurvedic medicine, Air is the force which governs the communication that must be activated in order for us to move our limbs, torso, head and neck as we bend over, stand up, reach, pull, push, walk, run, work, turn our heads, and swallow. With each physical action we take we are witnessing the influence of the Air Element.

Air's mobility flows in many directions: its inward and downward movement as we inhale; and its upward movement as we exhale and speak. Its constant flow draws nutrients in and out of our digestive tract and is the force behind the rhythmic movement involved in peristalsis. Its downward and outward flow assists in the processes of birth, menstruation and elimination. Its force governs the rhythm of our beating heart and regulates not only our blood flow but also the dilation and constriction of the blood vessels. It controls the movement of our muscles and joints to propel the motion of our body.

When the Air Element becomes aggravated in our body, often through improper diet and lifestyle, the precisely timed flow of our internal processes can spiral into a flurry of irregularity and disconnectedness resulting in ill-timed, out-of-sync communications. The once steady beat of the heart can quicken into an irregular rhythm of palpitations; blood pressure can quickly build and drastically shoot up, only to dangerously plunge once again; nerve transmissions can become confused and short-circuited as once graceful movement can turn into uncontrollable tremors.

When the air flow is weak in our body, we become sluggish and so do our body systems. The heartbeat can lose power and become slow; blood pressure can continually drop; we can experience poor circulation, sluggish bowels, and what was once easeful movement for us can turn into muscle stiffness, decreased motion, or even immobility.

Air can be blocked or trapped in our body. We can experience gas in our digestive system trying to escape in the form of hiccups, belching, bloating, or constipation. In more severe cases, blocked air in our system can lead to a lack – a lack of blood supply, a lack of oxygen or even tissue ischemia.

AIR IN OUR MIND

The natural inclination of Air is to steadily flow; to gently but assuredly give movement to our creativity and expression. Problems arise, however, when the flow in our mind becomes either too fast or too slow. When Air is unregulated or unimpeded, it can move in two ways. It can either lose its force, dissipate, and essentially blow itself out, or it can pick up speed – a tremendous amount of speed.

If the movement of the Air Element increases in our mind, it can lead to absolute chaos. It accelerates the sheer speed of our thoughts into an unimpeded creative flow. It swirls our creative processes into a maddening blur. We can't keep up with the unrelenting mental assault as our thoughts continually bombard us. We can easily become disorganized and restless. What's worse, it may lead to anxiety, worry, or even depression.

If, on the other hand, the flow of the Air Element is impeded or blocked in some way, not only will there be no propulsion of ideas and projects into the world, but the creative process itself may grind to a halt. The once free flowing stream of ideas may dry up. The once fertile mind may become barren. You may find you're unable to move forward creatively.

It is Air's mobile quality that propels creation. Its lightness encourages spontaneity, and its unpredictability lends itself to a dynamic personality. When the Air Element is regulated, its propulsive force allows thoughts and emotions to flow freely without accelerating out of control.

THE ACTION PLAN FOR THE ARTIST

While you certainly want to cultivate your creativity, if left unimpeded your creative stream has a tendency to accumulate speed and rush out of control. You'll want to regulate that flow and slow it down so you can manage it better and avoid anxiety or worry.

While you want to manage your flow of inspiration, you also want your creative stream to flow free of obstructions to avoid stagnancy. Without adequate propulsion your creative stream will dissipate, or perhaps even grind to a halt.

While you're a natural-born communicator, very social, and love to express yourself to others, you'll want to learn to manage and conserve your expressive energy so you don't become weak and depleted.

Your varied interests necessitate an agile mind, and perhaps cause you to multitask to keep all your projects in motion. You must, however, direct your energy and provide structure to your creative flow so your projects continue to move forward at a sure and steady pace.

TECHNIQUES FOR BRINGING THE ARTIST BACK INTO BALANCE

THINKING: In a word, think "calming." The Artist has a tendency to become very high strung. Direct your focus from the outside to the inside. Turn down the external stimuli by tuning into your breathing.

REGULATE YOUR BREATHING WITH THE THREE-PART BREATH: Since air itself naturally rises, the Artist can easily become overwhelmed with a busy mind trying to accommodate an excessive stream of incoming thoughts. Remember, the pace of your breath dictates the pace of your mind; if your breath is quick and shallow, your thoughts will become quick and shallow. Your breath is the leader here. Smoothing out the breath will put you back on track.

The pace of your breath will regulate the pace of your thoughts. Steady, deep and full breathing will ease and soothe the incoming mental stream. It will give you time to evaluate your thoughts and ideas, discard those which are irrelevant and give credence to those worth pursuing.

As the Zen Master Thich Nhat Hanh explains: "Breath is the bridge which connects life to consciousness, which unites your body to your thoughts. Whenever your mind becomes scattered, use your breath as the means to take hold of your mind again."[10]

The "Three-Part Breath" is a basic breathing sequence designed to calm your central nervous system. It releases tension and stress in the body while it also nourishes and relaxes you. It encourages you to calm the excess activity in your mind as you focus inward on your breath.[11]

TECHNIQUE: Part 1 - Sit cross-legged on the floor or you may lie on your back on the floor and empty your lungs of air. Begin your inhalation by focusing on your lower belly; the area below your navel. You can even place your hands on your belly to experience this part of the breath. As you inhale focus on the rise of your lower belly outward and the fall of your lower belly back in as you exhale.

Part 2 - Bring your attention to your middle as you inhale. You may place your hands on your ribs as you feel them flare out as you fill your lower lungs with air on the inhale, causing the ribs to widen apart and then return to normal on the exhale.

Part 3 - Focus on filling your upper chest right below your collar bones on the inhale and feel it deflate on the exhale. This is the heart center.

Now, string all the parts together as you make your inhale begin in your lower belly, then rise to flare out your ribs as you expand them outwards to either side, and then finish your inhale by sipping in a bit more air to fill out the upper chest. Exhale in the reverse order: one long exhale beginning with deflating your upper chest, then deflating your ribs inward, then deflating your lower belly as you draw your navel to your spine. Eventually the three parts will flow into each other naturally and smoothly, without pause. Continue at your own pace.

UNPLUG FROM TECHNOLOGY: Although the Artist is very social by nature and loves to communicate with others, they are particularly vulnerable to over-stimulation and must take measures to disconnect from the outside world for a bit, especially when they're feeling bombarded and overwhelmed.

The Artist is a multi-tasker by nature but can be easily overloaded by an onslaught of information. The more information you are bombarded with overstimulates the mind which can leave you exhausted and depleted. Ease into your day. Instead of checking your phone or email first thing in the morning or taking care of what's going on at work before you even arrive there, focus instead on taking care of yourself. We think by keeping things in plain view we're somehow managing them. This is not true. Constantly checking your phone and emails bleeds out your energy.

Designate a specific time frame every day to read and respond to messages. You'll know what to expect and work to answer them more efficiently because you know you have only designated a certain amount of time in which to get it all done. Also, manage your technology wisely. Turn off your computer and phone at least one or two hours before bedtime. Take charge and don't let technology run your life. Remember, if you don't manage it, it will certainly manage you.

BRING STRUCTURE TO YOUR LIFE: The Artist, like air itself, has an irregular nature – irregular in pace, rhythm, and intensity. Since like increases like, bringing even more irregularity into your lifestyle will throw you out of balance. Think of it this way: Unstructured energy leads to disorganization and chaos. While you're quite adaptable to new situations, consistency and direction is what actually serves you best.

In my estimation, the ultimate "structure guru" is Jo Frost; the Supernanny. It doesn't matter if you have young children or not. Consider the over-riding theme: bringing order to chaos. If you've ever watched an episode of Supernanny, you'll recall how Jo's efforts at creating a more structured home environment benefit everyone involved. Think about the behavior of an unruly child. At first, that child's energy will gain speed and momentum and very quickly escalate into total chaos. Eventually that child will expend his energy and dissipate it out, leaving themselves (and everyone around them) exhausted. To remedy the uncontrollable situation, Jo gives that child (and their energy) direction. She provides them with a much needed, healthy structure in which their attention can flow.

Artists take heed: in a more structured environment which shepherds your energy, your life will prosper from more regularity and your interests and projects will absolutely flourish. You will accomplish more without depleting your energy.

Create structure by making daily and nightly routines. Incorporating a routine of consistent practices throughout the day and evening will provide the Artist with regularity and an expectation of what is to take place. You will channel energy and effort into a consistent practice that will create reliability and calmness. Try to rise at the same time every morning. Also establish consistent times for meals and types of food you eat so your mind knows what to expect and won't have a jolt of surprise or struggle with indecision. Plan and schedule leisure time to pursue your interests and projects. Establish a consistent bedtime routine so the mind knows what to expect and where the evening is heading.

FEELING: Just like air, the Artist's true nature is free flowing movement. The key, however, is to ensure that the movement continues in a steady flow, but does not swirl into a destructive spiral, derailing the Artist. To remain in balance, you must be able to channel your expression without getting winded or wound up. You would greatly benefit from channeling this excess energy downward, out of your head and into your body to return to a state of calm. The way to bring the Artist into balance is to channel their movement into a slower, steadier pace.

LINK THE BREATH WITH MOVEMENT: We spend most of our time with our mind going one way, and our body going another way. Really integrating the mind and the body takes focus. Mind/Body practices bring awareness to our movement and focus our mind. Linking your breath with your movement is a way to bring you into the present moment as you practice mindfulness. When you're really in the present moment there is no room for extraneous thoughts. When you slow down your movement, you slow down your mind, and the body begins to regulate itself. You breathe more fully. Moving with your breath encourages more graceful and deliberate movement and it promotes a steady flow both physically and mentally.

The Artist will find this slower, more contemplative and intentional form of movement in disciplines like Tai Chi, Qi Gong and Yoga to be exceptionally beneficial to both mind and body. The key is in linking breath with movement. It isn't difficult to link breath with movement, but it does take practice. Conscious breathing activates the parasympathetic nervous system (PNS) and triggers a corresponding drop in heart rate. It also acts to suppress stress hormones, like adrenaline and cortisol, in the bloodstream. When the breath deepens, the lungs expand. The message is conveyed to the brain to tell the muscles that it is safe to relax. The beauty of these universal disciplines is that you can tailor them to your own body and experience level.

Linking breath with movement requires a concerted effort and focus, but the results are transformative and profound; especially to the Artist. Without the relationship between breath and movement, you're simply raising and lowering your limbs and bending forwards and backwards without awareness. When you're mindful of the breath as you move, you maximize your movements and you tune out distractions.

I have consistently practiced yoga for over 20 years now and, although my yoga path has led me to many different teachers and styles, I will never forget my first introduction to this amazing and transformative practice. My teacher, Renee, began the class by asking if I knew what yoga was. When I answered "no," she proceeded to demonstrate. She told me to make a fist with my one hand. As I did, she instructed me to squeeze it tighter . . . then tighter . . . and even tighter still. She made me hold my clenched fist very still until my forearm and fist were totally exhausted from the force and I could barely squeeze my fist any longer. She then instructed me to slowly release my fist and observe my open palm. I felt the rush of relief immediately. I felt like I was being kind to myself by releasing my grip, finally ending the suffering I was causing. I witnessed the color begin to return, I felt the blood flow rush in as it naturally wanted and needed to do – and how I was preventing that from happening – and the circulation return my hand back to life. I felt like I had stopped punishing myself with the grip of my own hand. As I looked at Renee for guidance as to what I had just witnessed, she pointed to my rejuvenated open fist and exclaimed "That is yoga!"

As my yoga practice has grown since that time, I can tell you that in addition to increasing my strength and flexibility, yoga provides me with a way to still my mind; a way to make me present; quiet my thoughts; tap into my body with greater awareness, and to remember to breathe. It is calming, yet enlivening; precisely how we want to balance the Artist.

EASY STRETCHING: Try to incorporate the following simple stretches into your evening activities, or perhaps as part of your bedtime ritual. These stretches will calm anxiety and nervousness as you wind down from your busy day. They will help you to release tension, untie knotted muscles, and unblock tight areas, physically and mentally. On another level, the Artist can see that positive results can come from doing less, not more.[12]

STANDING FORWARD FOLD: Stand with your feet about shoulder-width apart. Inhale with your arms above your head; as if you're reaching for the sky. Keeping your back as straight as you can, hinge from your waist as you fold forward on your exhale. Let your hands rest on your shins or ankles, whichever is available to you, and relax your head and neck. Let gravity assist the lengthening of your spine. Bend as far forward as you comfortably can without straining. Try to gently straighten your knees to the extent you are able, without locking them. Let your head hang from the root of your neck. Close your eyes and take long, slow, deep breaths in and out of your nose. As you inhale, observe any tightness or tension in your body; and on the exhale let those areas loosen and release. Visualize those tight areas melting away into relaxation. Continue breathing and relaxing for as long as you can tolerate the stretch. To release from the stretch, slowly roll up one vertebra at a time, letting your head be the last thing to come up. Stand quietly for a few breaths, and just observe how your body feels.

SITTING FORWARD FOLD: If your lower back is tight or if you are nursing a low back injury, try the seated version of Forward Fold which will still have value for grounding you and easing your nervous system. Relax your body into this pose rather than force yourself into it.

Sit on the floor with your legs straight out in front of you. Bring both arms up parallel to your ears as you inhale. Stretch your spine as you raise your arms up toward the sky, then lean forward from your hips as you exhale, keeping your spine and legs as straight as you can tolerate. Draw your chest as close to your thighs as possible. Hold for approximately 30 seconds, or shorter if you can't tolerate the stretch. Inhale as you stretch up again and repeat two to three times.[13]

Forward folds encourage the downward flow of energy into the body which is vital to balancing the Artist's busy mind. Actually, forward folding calms the nervous system by creating a sense of "safety"; similar to a fetal position. Remember that in forward folds, you are compressing and massaging your abdominal organs, which will help in digestion and elimination.

LEGS UP THE WALL*: Place a mat or blanket on the floor just below where you will be placing your legs on the wall. Lie on your side and place your buttocks as close as possible to where the floor and the wall meet. Using your core muscles and hips, turn onto your back and stretch your legs straight up along the wall. Arrange yourself so you are resting at a 90-degree angle – with your back fully on the floor and your legs outstretched on the wall. You may relax your arms by your sides, or place them on your belly, or stretch them out to the sides to form a T and close your eyes. Slowly count to 5 as you inhale, and count to 5 as you exhale. Hold this pose for as long as you like as you continue to release tension. To come out of the pose, gently bend your knees towards your chest and roll to one side. Rest there for several breaths. Then press your hands into the floor and walk yourself up to sitting, let your head come up last. Sit quietly for a few minutes and feel the effects.

To alleviate any strain you may feel, you can place a pillow or a towel under your lower back, or head, depending on what is optimal for your comfort.

Legs up the wall provides a quick relief from stress and anxiety. Added benefits are that it is a great stretch for the hips and leg muscles including hamstrings and calves. It relieves swelling in the legs and feet, and it helps to alleviate low back pain. It's called an "inversion" pose, meaning that it inverts the typical actions of our lower body as we most often sit or stand all day long.[14]

Do not perform this stretch if you have glaucoma, hypertension, or a hernia.

ACTIVITIES THAT CONSIST OF FLUID, REPETITIVE MOVEMENT: If you'd like to incorporate even more movement into your life, consider activity that is enjoyable to you and that involves fluid, repetitive movements like walking, easy bicycling, rowing or swimming. These types of activities won't bombard the body or mind with excess stimulation, constant stopping and starting, or irregular movements. Fluid and repetitive motion will work to calm and balance the tense and anxious propensities of the Artist.

EATING: To balance out the Artist's tendency toward irregular digestion, make sure the food you consume is warm (in temperature and energetically) in order to soothe, relax, and calm your body. Since air is naturally light, the Artist must balance this inherent quality with food that is more substantial and heavier in texture. And to provide a welcome counterbalance to their tendencies to dry out, accumulate speed, and move in an irregular fashion, the Artist should adopt specific cooking techniques when preparing meals.

WARMING FOODS AND BEVERAGES: Lean toward hot, creamy cereals like oatmeal, cream of rice, cream of wheat, or quinoa; and treats like rice pudding, bread pudding, warm and comforting fruit pies, and cobblers. Incorporate warming spices like cinnamon, nutmeg, ginger, cardamom and cloves as part of your meal ingredients and preparations; or drink them alone or in combination in the form of hot teas. You can sip the tea in the morning with breakfast, throughout the day, or in the evening before bedtime.

FOOD THAT IS MODERATELY HEAVY IN TEXTURE AND HAS DEPTH OF FLAVOR: To counterbalance the naturally thin quality of air, the Artist will greatly benefit by eating foods that are a little thicker in texture. Favor thicker sauces, broths, and soups like old-fashioned chicken and rice, or tasty carrot with ginger, or perhaps creamy butternut squash with fennel. Add heartier and satisfying vegetables to your diet like cooked beets, fresh corn, acorn squash, and potatoes. Other good options to incorporate into your diet are olives, soft cheeses, and eggs.

Create depth in your seasoning. To create a depth of flavor for the Artist, make sure to eat food that is in season; when its flavor is at its peak. Use flavorful stock over water in your cooking when possible. Chicken stock, beef stock, or vegetable stock provide significantly more flavor than plain water. Adding a squeeze of lemon juice, a sprinkle of lemon zest, or a splash of apple cider vinegar may add just the needed punch to wake up the flavor of your meal. Fresh herbs should be favored whenever possible. If you should only have dried herbs available, place the dried herbs in a mesh sieve and press down on them to release their flavorful oils. Remember that good quality oils like olive oil, sesame oil, and ghee add tremendous flavor to your food.

ADOPT MOIST, SLOW, AND EVEN COOKING METHODS TO COUNTERBALANCE THE AIR ELEMENT'S TENDENCIES TOWARDS DRYNESS, SPEED AND IRREGULARITY. Moist cooking methods will help to compensate for the dry quality of the Air Element. Employ techniques like braising. Cooking meat and/or veggies slowly in a liquid medium makes for richer and more complex flavors, and a thicker sauce; and it yields powerfully flavored food. Other moist cooking techniques include pot roasting, poaching, and steaming.

Slow cooking methods will help to equalize air's tendency to pick up speed. Avoid flash frying or quick, deep frying. Instead, use a slow cooker to create some mouth-watering, comforting stews and casseroles. The centering concept of one-pot meals, where ingredients and flavors are melded together, also serves as a great counterpoise to the formless and often haphazard qualities of the Air Element.

Even cooking methods will help to counteract air's irregular nature. Aim for preparations that call for cooking at a lower, even temperature and result in even doneness. For example, while a stir-fry can be delicious, it generally requires an uneven cooking method – cooking the thicker ingredients first, then adding in the other ingredients at different times. Rather, consistency in temperature, doneness and texture serves the Artist best.

The Transformer

DOES THE TRANSFORMER SOUND LIKE YOU?

It's the Transformer who always takes the lead. Their brilliant intellect and their ability to grasp ideas quickly and easily gain the trust and admiration of those around them. The Transformer processes information very quickly, and they're able to accurately cut to the chase in record time. Whether they're advocating their own position in a one-on-one conversation with a friend, or arguing a case in front of a jury, the Transformer constantly fuels whatever they're doing with intensity, passion and articulate expression.

ATTRIBUTES:
- Are you naturally competitive?
- Do you grasp and process information quickly?
- Do you perform well under pressure?
- Are you ambitious?
- Do you enjoy the process of turning theory into practice?

YET, PERHAPS:
- Do you have a tendency to become critical of yourself and of those around you?
- Do you draw conclusions quickly, sometimes unfairly?
- Do you have a sharp tongue when others don't meet your expectations?

If you answered "yes" to most of these questions, then you naturally align most closely with the Fire Element. You want to fuel your transformative nature but keep it balanced as well. Since the Transformer's strength lies in their ability to digest and process information, the key to balancing the Transformer is through their digestive fire. It governs their digestion of food as well as their digestion of thoughts, feelings and emotions. Keeping the Transformer's mental and physical digestive fire burning brightly, yet contained, is the goal. Focus your attention on enkindling the fire itself, but paying attention to the "fuel" you throw on the fire is of equal importance.

A REAL-LIFE TRANSFORMER

In the Spring of 1992, I was hired by a small law firm to manage the discovery phase of a very large construction litigation case for one of their clients. At that time, I was a young attorney not only looking for mentors in my career, but in search of a "juicy" case to sink my teeth into. It turned out that I found both.

This particular litigation involved the anchor tenant of a downtown Pittsburgh skyscraper suing the Madison Avenue architects for their "inferior design," as well as the general contractor, and the various engineering firms for numerous structural and mechanical deficiencies. While these particular defendants pointed their fingers at one another they also, in turn, pointed their fingers at the bevy of sub-contractors on the project who were joined as additional defendants, one of whom was our client.

As you can imagine, skyscrapers are like bustling mini-cities in and of themselves. And, as in any mini-city, many, *many* things can go wrong. True to form, in this particular case they did, from the steel panel "curtain wall" design, to the quality of glass, to the neoprene gaskets used in the windows, to the exterior paint, to the internal plumbing, to the HVAC systems, even to the underground snow-melt cable. And that's just an abridged list of the highlights.

The firm that hired me represented the smallest sub-contractor who was the manufacturer of a gas-safety shut off valve which, for all intents and purposes, precisely did its job and functioned in the exact manner it was supposed to. Turns out, late one evening, when for whatever reason the gas pressure in the building exceeded its flow speed, the guillotine mechanism in the valve immediately descended, effectively shutting off the excessive flow of gas to the entire building. The only problem was that this occurred at a very late hour on Christmas Eve in sub-zero weather. Almost no one was in the 55-story structure and, by the time anyone even caught on that something may be amiss, the ripple effect had already created tremendous issues. But we had a solid defense and entered the deposition room pointing our own fingers, while taking a relatively demure seat among our "additional defendant" colleagues.

Since my job was to tend to the discovery phase of this litigation, the majority of my workday was spent attending depositions; depositions that were scheduled every day, all day long, for about ten months straight in the plaintiffs' attorneys' downtown offices. Representing the smallest additional defendant in all this mayhem allowed me the opportunity to sit back and observe while the others battled it out. I suppose at times you could call it boring, particularly when blue prints were unrolled all across the conference room table, but for the most part, my role and responsibilities were the answer to what I had been looking for up to this point in my legal career.

Each party was represented by a virtual "who's who" of Pittsburgh's legal elite; each attorney called upon at different times to showcase their various legal styles and skills, all the while vigorously representing (either questioning on behalf of or in defense of) their respective clients. It was a litigator's dream come true – at least this young litigator's dream come true! There I was, taking my rightful seat at the table, amongst the well-known and highly respected names of the local legal society, watching ringside as they "duked it out." I loved my job!

There were two attorneys, however, I wasn't initially familiar with, who represented the general contractor (the target Defendant) in this litigation. They worked for a law firm just outside of New York City which specialized in construction defense litigation. I came to learn that just about every attorney in this firm had an engineering degree. These two attorneys flew into Pittsburgh every Monday morning for the work week on the case and flew back to New York City every Friday evening for the weekend. The older attorney, Gene, was a well experienced partner in the firm, and the other, Nick, was a younger associate. Turns out, Nick was only a couple years older than I was.

Nick was the one who took charge of the case. Gene came along to attend the first few initial depositions and appeared for the more major players who were being deposed; mostly to get the "lay of the land," sense the tone of the room, and become acquainted with the personalities involved.

Although still considered a "young attorney," Nick carried himself with an air of someone much more experienced. In a word, he was sharp. I remember he wore the most beautiful Hermès ties, impeccably knotted, and high-quality tailored suits. The way he defended his own client, and questioned other parties' representatives, was like watching a master at work. His questions were incisive and discerning. He had a complete grasp of the facts and he knew where the weak spots were. He was polished and articulate. He commanded the room and the respect of everyone in it.

Although Nick may not have logged in as many "lawyering" years as the others seated at the table had, the field of construction law was his forté, and no one doubted that he knew what he was doing. While his client in this case was the target defendant, Nick's talents were on display. His questions, and his manner, let you know that this was his specialty. From the perspective of a young female attorney, he was charismatic. To sum it all up, he exuded confidence, and he had the skills and knowledge to back it all up to boot.

I don't know if it was admiration for his legal skills, or a full-blown crush I had on him – likely a little of both. Hey, aside from learning interesting tidbits of information from the deposition testimony (like that Tnemec paint is the word "cement" spelled backwards) watching my new crush gave me another reason to get up and go to work every day.

There were many times when Nick and Gene (when he was in attendance) became impatient with the other attorneys in the room. I remember one day in particular, I had, in my mind, one of the coveted seats next to Gene around the large oval conference room table. The morning literally dragged as we listened to an exceptionally long and drawn out exchange of questions and answers between one of the defense attorneys and the main architect for the skyscraper. Gene became increasingly frustrated and perturbed as the morning went on because the defense attorney spent a tremendous amount of time dwelling on the witness's high school education, his hobbies, and his family.

After Gene raised an inordinate number of "objection to relevance" calls, I noticed that he began to lean over towards me as he started to speak. "Let me point something out to you . . ." he began. I eagerly leaned in closer to gather up the anticipated "pearls of wisdom" I was about to receive. My mind blocked out all the other sounds in the room as I awaited his next words. He proceeded with his advice in an intentionally not so quiet "whisper" so the others sitting around the table could hear: " . . . if you can't distill into two hours what you want to ask a witness, you don't know what you're doing." While his intent was more to express his frustration about what was unfolding in front of us more so than to provide guidance to a young attorney, to this day – some 26 years later – I still remember that advice.

Nick learned well. His skills bespoke of his mentor's teachings. As the months went on, Nick and I became more closely acquainted. Near the end of the case when all the attorneys were working diligently towards framing a settlement, my boss decided to take my place and become more involved. One morning as everyone was mulling around outside the courtroom before a settlement conference, Nick deliberately walked up to my boss and asked: "What are you doing here? Lisa is so much better received than you are."

That case finally settled (likely from its own weight). Having busy schedules, other clients to represent, and careers to build, we each went our separate ways. Since that time, I have taken a look (or many) to find out what trajectory Nick's career took. Shortly after the case ended, Nick opened up his own law firm. He has since established himself, and his firm, as nationally recognized leaders in construction litigation and real estate transactions. He has authored numerous articles and has spoken to audiences across the country. His law firm has grown as well; he opened a satellite office a few years ago. It's no wonder to me. I would expect nothing less from Nick in light of his tremendous drive and intelligence.

MORE ABOUT THE FIRE ELEMENT

The Fire Element manifests in our body by fueling all of our metabolic and chemical actions such as digestion, metabolism, maintaining temperature, and comprehension. The Fire Element is also responsible for transforming what we see into visual impressions. It metabolizes what we take into our body, from the food we eat to the thoughts we think, to our sensory experiences. When it burns brightly and efficiently, the Fire Element discerns the quality of all that we ingest, extracts and absorbs that which will nourish our body and mind, and discards the waste which will not serve us well.

FIRE AS INITIATING CHANGE

It may be 93 million miles away from us but the sun—the ultimate fire in our universe—is the main source of energy for life on Earth. The sun's heat warms our waters and drives our weather patterns.

The sun also plays an integral role in the process of photosynthesis – along with water and carbon dioxide – to enable plants to manufacture their own food (glucose) that the plant cells can use as energy to grow and mature.[15]

Natural sunlight initiates changes that occur in our own body. When we expose our body to sunlight our skin manufactures Vitamin D, the vitamin (or hormone) so necessary to prevent autoimmune disease and which absorbs calcium from our intestinal tract to be used for building healthy bones and teeth.[16]

FIRE AS LIBERATING

Fire is the means by which energy is liberated from its source. When we cook food, heat breaks apart the chemical bonds which knit food together. Cooked food yields more energy because the heating process releases more vitamins and minerals from our food. More nutrients are bioavailable for our body to assimilate.

The process of cooking also makes food easier for us to chew and digest. It lessens our need to exclusively call upon our own enzymatic activity to do the digesting for us. In other words, consuming cooked food helps us to conserve our own energy; energy we would otherwise expend "cooking" raw food in our own "internal fire."

FIRE AS CONVERTING

We convert sunlight into power by harnessing the Sun's radiant light and heat to generate electricity. Solar panels, which are a collection of individual photovoltaic cells, absorb light. Through a semi-conductor, the absorbed light is converted into electricity. Solar thermal technology uses heat from the Sun to create steam. The steam spins a turbine, which is connected to a generator. The generator then creates electricity.[17]

FIRE AS TRANSFORMATION, AND REBIRTH

The story of the Phoenix – also known as the "Fire Bird" – is often associated with the sun and is a wonderful representation of transformation and rebirth through fire. According to the Ancient Greek legend, the Phoenix lives for hundreds of years. When it senses it is at the end of its lifespan, it makes a nest of cinnamon, sage and myrrh and it sets itself on fire. It is from the ashes of the fire that the bird rises again to live another span of several hundred years.[18]

Fire has the ability to transform the nature and substance of any raw materials we feed it. As we all know, the food we feed our body is transformed by the fire of our digestive system into our physical structure. It is equally important to understand that the thoughts, feelings and emotions we feed our mind are ignited and transformed by the fire of our comprehension into our world views and life perspectives.

FIRE AS ILLUMINATING

On a practical level, fire can be used as illumination to enable our eyes to see and to navigate our way. On a metaphorical level, the Fire Element sheds light on new ideas and sets ablaze our comprehension, perception and understanding. It also lights the way for us to change our perspectives.

We use phrases like: "It came to light," or "It dawned on me," to show the power of Fire's revelatory nature. The "Age of Enlightenment" is yet another example of the influence of the Fire Element which led to a rejection of traditional religious and social ideas in favor of a world view based upon reason, logic and skepticism.

FIRE IN THE BODY

The Fire Element has an affinity for our digestive system. The heat of our digestive fire literally burns the form of the food we ingest and transforms it into nutrients our body can use. It is through the heating process of enzymatic activity that the sum and substance of what we feed ourselves turns into how we are nourished.

When our digestive fire is performing at its peak, we feel light and engaged. We experience balanced energy throughout the day. Our body is strong and our mind is sharp. Our skin glows and our eyes shine brightly.

If the Fire Element begins to rage out of control, however, the luster of the skin may fade and erupt into severe rashes; the once bright eyes may turn bloodshot; tissues may become inflamed; heartburn or fever may be present; and the once efficient-running metabolism may turn hyper-acidic. Our body will attempt to regulate the excess heat as we sweat more, urinate more, and as our stools become looser and more frequent.

Issues manifest as well if the internal Fire Element is weak, or even extinguished. That once-glowing skin may turn dull, and the body will attempt to hold on to as much heat as possible to keep its systems functioning. In that case, our sweating decreases, we don't urinate as much, and we may experience constipation because we won't eliminate from our bowels as much or as frequently.

FIRE IN THE MIND

Fire naturally burns hot and bright. Its heat must remain enkindled, yet not burn out of control. When the Fire Element burns out of control in the mind, our words can turn biting and scorch those around us. A once discerning intellect can melt into judgment; confidence may explode into arrogance or egotism; the desire for efficiency can smolder as impatience; passion can ignite into fanaticism; and unmet expectations can burn away, leaving behind the ashes of anger and resentment.

You may find yourself enraged at someone's slight misstep. You may lash out in anger with a sharp tongue that cuts up one side and down the other. You might judge, belittle, or snap at someone with little regard for their feelings. These types of reactions represent the Fire Element burning out of control in the mind.

If the Fire Element is weak, however, we can't easily process new information. The once razor sharp intellect with a strong appetite to consume information now becomes dull. Confidence wanes, and passion turns noncommittal.

When it's in balance and under control, the flames of the Fire Element illuminate our comprehension and set our intellect ablaze with curiosity and insight. Its heat ignites our intellect; it fuels confidence; it refines our efficiency; it intensifies our passion; it focuses our attention and helps us to readily "burn through" data and churn out results.

THE ACTION PLAN FOR THE TRANSFORMER

You want to make sure your physical digestion remains strong to completely metabolize the food you ingest into your body so that no toxins are left behind to decay. You also want to ensure your emotional digestion is working at its peak performance to properly assimilate thoughts and feelings without leaving any "emotional residue" behind to fester.

You want to keep your radiant intellect burning brightly so you can properly discern and articulate your ideas, thoughts, feelings and emotions.

You want to pay particular attention to what kind of "fuel" you're feeding yourself, not only physically, but also the fuel you're feeding the fire of your intellect. Make sure you're ingesting quality "food," in the proper quantity, for your body as well as for your senses.

Be aware of how hot your digestive flame burns, lest it rage out of control. Properly tending to your digestive fire is essential for your body, to prevent hyper-acidity, as well as for your mind, to avoid scorching those around you with anger, criticism and judgment.

TECHNIQUES FOR BRINGING THE TRANSFORMER BACK INTO BALANCE

THINKING: Proper digestion does not just refer to the food we eat. The concept of someone with healthy, strong digestion expands to include the thorough digestion, absorption, and assimilation of our thoughts, feelings and emotions. Much like the end result of proper physical digestion is vibrant physical health, the end result of proper mental digestion is proper understanding, accurate perspectives and healthy relationships. If our mental digestive fire is impaired, then our thoughts, feelings and emotions are improperly digested and create mental toxins.

We take in so much information through our five senses that the input must be managed well. We also have to turn inward and take inventory of our own emotional health. Introspection will help us clean out what may be emotionally overloading us. It's also crucial that we live in balance with Nature's rhythms as we work towards balance in our own lives. Going against natural rhythms puts undue stress on us and can overload our circuits. Living in harmony with Nature's rhythms automatically balances our own natural rhythms.

MAKE AN HONEST ASSESSMENT OF THE QUALITY AND QUANTITY OF YOUR TYPICAL SENSORY INPUT AND CHANGE IT IF NECESSARY.

SIGHT: What kinds of news stories, television programs or movies are you watching? Are they violent? Disturbing? Are people fighting or in distress? A constant stream of these types of images puts you at risk for chronic stress and increased health issues.[19]

By focusing on peaceful, calming images, your body actually bathes in soothing neurotransmitters. So, switch off the violence and intensity and tune in to an interesting documentary, or a topic you're drawn to that will enhance your knowledge and skills.

HEARING: What are you listening to on the radio? What kinds of ideas are the radio talk shows or podcasts promoting? What kind of music are you listening to? What are the lyrics conveying? Is the volume turned up too high? What about other people around you? Are their words mean or hurtful? I used to work in a law firm where my co-workers always spoke in terms of "lack," always speaking of themselves in terms of "below" the level of others in the firm. Those comments used to hit me like a punch in the stomach. Consider any kind of noise pollution – whether it is an assault in audibility or in substance – a threat to your well-being. It can lead to stress and an impaired immune system.[20]

Make it a point to listen to something that soothes your ears, whether it is beautiful music or inspirational words, that leave you feeling uplifted and happy. When you incorporate these sounds or messages into your daily routine, pleasure-producing chemicals course through your body which support your overall health.

SMELL: What kind of air are you breathing? Are you able to get outside and breathe fresh air at all? Do you open the windows where you live? Our sense of smell (olfaction) is our most primitive sense. The olfactory system is located in our brain, so the sense of smell is closely related to emotions, memory, and mood.[21] Try incorporating essential oils into your routine. Try scents that are cooling or calming like sandalwood, rose or peppermint.

TASTE: What often greets your tastebuds? Is it processed food laden with "excitotoxins" that overload your tastebuds with a distorted, artificial taste? Do you regularly eat out, consume junk food, fast food, or soda pop? Do you often eat highly flavored snacks or processed foods? If so, it's very likely you're consuming a steady stream of excitotoxins which includes MSG or aspartame. Excitotoxins overstimulate our body.[22]

Switch up your diet by stopping the intake of processed foods and incorporate more antioxidant rich foods like organically grown fresh fruits and vegetables.

TOUCH: Do you take good care of your skin? Or is it dry and cracked? Our skin is the body's largest organ and ensuring that it is in good condition is essential to our health. It is also the largest barrier we have against infection. Keeping our skin clean and moist helps to maintain its integrity. Using oils like sesame or coconut to moisturize is an excellent way to ensure your skin is getting proper nutrients and remains strong and supple. [23]

TURN YOUR FOCUS INWARD AND PRACTICE INTROSPECTION: Introspection – the act of reflectively looking inward – is an effective tool to help the Transformer sort through their thoughts and emotions.

Routine emotional cleansing is like routinely keeping a clean house. If you keep accumulating things in your house without sorting through them, you eventually run out of room. You then begin to precariously stack one thing on top of another, without rhyme or reason, and without a solid foundation; scattered and haphazard. The same holds true with our emotions. If you don't "sort through" them in a timely manner and throw out the ones that do not serve you well, they become overcrowded in your mind. In order to find room as more present themselves to you, you begin to stuff everything into the corners and recesses of your mind. And when it comes down to it, you won't be able to find proper emotional responses when you need them.

Pay attention to your thoughts, feelings and emotions. Pay attention to your reactions to others. Can you witness yourself react before you do so out loud? Try to be the witness to yourself in a non-judgmental way. Self-reflection is a positive form of introspection. It causes us to accept our short-comings, learn from our missteps, and move forward with much more awareness. Be careful, however, not to self-ruminate.[24] Don't obsess over your thoughts, identify with your behaviors and justify your reactions.

HONOR THE RHYTHMS OF NATURE AS YOU MOVE TO BALANCE YOUR LIFE: Nature's rhythms will help to optimize our daily activities of sleeping, awakening and working. It takes great effort to resist nature's forces. Try swimming against the tide or running headlong into a hurricane force wind. Although, some of nature's forces aren't always visible to us. Nature also exerts much more subtle forces that we can't see, but if we're aware of them we can certainly feel their effects. Actually, we're often struggling against these forces, but we don't realize it. When we become aware of nature's rhythms and live accordingly, our life will flow much more smoothly.

In a daily cycle, there is a weighted energy that dominates from 6 a.m. to 10 a.m. that allows us to awaken in a calm state and helps to ground us as we get ready for our day. That's why it is best to awaken and rise by 6 a.m. If you do so any later, you'll be struggling against the natural force of heaviness and it will be much more difficult to awaken and get your day started.

Between 10 a.m and 2 p.m. a more intense and active energy takes over that helps to promote more physical and mental activity as it helps increase our productivity. This intensity assists our processes of digesting, metabolizing and distributing our energy. It keeps us alert and functioning at our peak performance for doing our daily activities. This is also a good time to tackle problems head on; to address them, analyze them, and move towards resolving them.

Between 2 p.m. and 6 p.m. a different energy influences us that begins to lighten our intensity and broaden our perspective. This time of the day allows us to take a step back from the problems and issues we were able to discern and contemplate a few hours earlier and assists us in designing creative solutions to them. We approach our tasks with freshness and ingenuity at this time.

As our nightly cycle begins, there is an energy of heaviness once again between 6 p.m. and 10 p.m. that helps us to wind down our busy day and settle in for a restful night's sleep. Utilize this window of time in the evening to finish up projects and activities, and engage in calming practices to allow this energy to help you drift off to sleep, preferably by 10 p.m.

From 10 p.m. to 2 a.m., we experience another round of active energy but, unlike the daily cycle which focused this energy outward, the active night energy during this time turns inward as it works on the internal cleansing of our body. That's why it is important that you are already asleep during this time, so you allow your body to cleanse properly and completely.

There is an energy of movement between 2 a.m. and 6 a.m. that fosters a sense of stimulation and lightness in us. This more invigorating energy will help us to awaken from our sleep. You may notice that it is difficult to go back to a sound sleep if you awaken during this time. Try to get out of bed by 6 a.m. to reap the benefits of this energy of movement to get you started for the day.

FEELING: The whole idea behind good, strong digestion is to completely burn what we ingest so that the proper nutrients are extracted to nourish our body as well as our mind, and the waste is completely separated and eliminated so that no toxic residue is left behind. The best way to ensure our digestion is strong is to keep our internal digestive flame enkindled and burning brightly.

RISE AND SET EATING: Pattern your eating according to the rising and setting of the sun – the ultimate fire in our universe. The increase and decrease of the sun's intensity throughout the day mirrors the natural intensity of our own internal digestive fire. Use it as a template for optimum eating.

As the sun rises in the morning, we can begin to feel its warmth, and sense its brightness. Therefore, your breakfast should be light, nutritious and satisfying; nothing heavy in quantity or texture so as to mirror the weaker, yet awakening power of our own digestion. At midday, the sun is at its peak in intensity. To optimize your own digestive fire, eat your largest meal at midday when your body's digestive system is functioning at its own full strength. In the early evening, the sun is setting, and its brightness is waning. Keep your evening meal light, nutritious, and satisfying so you don't overtax the waning intensity of your own digestive fire during this time.[25]

MAKE SURE TO CHEW YOUR FOOD WELL: Although this advice may sound insignificant, do not underestimate its powerful effect. Think of it this way, smaller wood chips thrown into a fire burn more readily than a big log does. By breaking up your food into smaller pieces in your mouth as you chew, you are ensuring that your digestive fire can more completely burn them rather than expending more of its energy breaking them down itself. This will make your digestive fire operate more efficiently to ensure that you derive the most benefit from your food with the least amount of toxic residue left behind.[26]

AVOID CONSUMING COLD FOOD OR BEVERAGES: Remember, our digestive fire is like any other fire – it is hot and fluid. It grows and it wanes in its need. It is bright – it increases and decreases in its intensity. It has the capacity to destroy and transform.

We want to keep our digestive fire strong and burning brightly so it can carry out its functions. We don't want any interruption in this process that will leave food undigested. Food that remains undigested will ferment and turn toxic in our system. It is this toxicity that is the root cause of disease in the body. We want to enkindle our digestive fire, not stomp it out.

When we consume food or beverages that are cold, chilled, iced or frozen, we are stopping our digestive process in its tracks. The coldness itself will immediately stifle our digestive fire. Its strength will begin to diminish at that point, and it will take much more energy and time to warm it up enough to resume its normal digestive capabilities. Commonly after drinking cold water or consuming cold food and beverages people develop stomach cramps and discomfort. They may also experience bloating, sluggishness, or a decrease in appetite. It is best to consume food and beverages that are room temperature, warm or hot.

EATING: To balance out the Transformer's hot nature and their tendency towards inflammation and over-acidity, emphasize foods that are energetically cooling as well as alkalizing. Adding in bitter tasting foods will be very beneficial to the Transformer. These foods will clear excess heat, purify the blood, and support the liver. Remember, the liver is the organ that energetically stores up anger – which is often a default emotion for the Transformer and one which they must learn to rein in and manage well.

FOOD THAT IS ENERGETICALLY COOLING IS KEY FOR THE TRANSFORMER: Hot and spicy tastes will aggravate the already heated tendencies of the Transformer. Steer clear of Cayenne, Curry Powder, Raw Garlic, and Horseradish which will aggravate the Transformer's already hot and spicy nature.

Energetically cooling vegetables like asparagus, green beans, cucumber, and zucchini; cooling fruits like apples, coconut, melons, strawberries and raspberries; and cooling herbs like cilantro, coriander (which is the seed form of cilantro), fennel and mint will all serve the Transformer well in their efforts to balance out their tendency to overheat.

ALKALIZING FOODS FOR BALANCE: Alkalizing foods are especially good for the Transformer to eat in order to balance out their tendency towards acidity. By their very nature, Transformers tend to be intense, stressed and focused. It's easy to grab for coffee, candy, a sugary "pick me up" or even excess animal protein as they pour so much energy into their work and other pursuits.

Be cautious of consuming too many acidic foods and beverages. Some of the most highly acid forming substances include pharmaceutical drugs, artificial sweeteners, processed food made with refined flour and refined sugar, coffee, alcohol and soft drinks. When we consume acidic food and /or beverages, the body tries to neutralize all that acid by releasing our store of alkaline minerals in an effort to balance out the internal environment we created. Alkaline forming minerals include potassium, magnesium, calcium, and sodium. If our alkaline minerals stores are empty, the body will pull or leech those minerals anywhere it can find them - primarily from our bones. The danger occurs when our body has leeched out all of our mineral reserves in its effort to neutralize the acidic onslaught we give it.

When the acid load is too overwhelming and our body doesn't have the resources to neutralize it, we store the excess acid in our connective tissues including muscles, tendons, ligaments and collagen fibers which will lead to inflammation. We'll begin to experience conditions like arthritis or fibromyalgia. So, our focus is really two-fold, curbing our acid consumption and bolstering our alkaline reserve.[27]

Avoid soda pop and junk food. Incorporate alkalizing foods into your daily meals. Consume greens, like spinach, kale, or beet tops. Add avocados, celery and cucumbers to a salad. Steam or roast some broccoli, cauliflower, or brussels sprouts.

THE BENEFITS OF BITTER TASTING FOODS: While bitter tasting foods won't provide you with a feeling of satisfaction from eating them, they will, however, stimulate your palate (and your appetite) to search out more satisfying tastes. Bitter tasting foods will assist in digestion as well. Bitter foods are cooling to the system and work as anti-inflammatories for the body. They are also some of the best blood purifies around because they cleanse and support the liver.[28]

The Transformer can add the bitter taste to their diet in the form of bitter greens – like arugula, endive, radicchio, dandelion greens and collards. Even dark chocolate embodies the bitter taste because of the higher concentration of cocoa, while also having a lower sugar content than sweet chocolate. Remember, as you add the bitter taste into your diet, do so in small amounts. Even in small doses, the bitter taste delivers powerful flavor.

The Pacifist

DOES THE PACIFIST SOUND LIKE YOU?

It's usually the Pacifist who can get along with just about everyone. Their compassionate nature and ability to bring people together set them up for their role in the center. They iron out the wrinkles, smooth ruffled feathers, and help adversaries see eye to eye, or at the very least help them to respect each other's viewpoint. Although we may not readily notice it, the smooth functioning of any group can usually look to a Pacifist at the helm, ensuring smooth sailing ahead.

ATTRIBUTES:
- Do you have a calming nature?
- Can you generally see all sides of an argument?
- Do your friends and family feel comfortable coming to you with their problems?
- Are you naturally inclined to be the protector?
- Do you have a knack for keeping relationships or tasks on track?

YET, PERHAPS:
- Can you become overly protective to the point of smothering?
- Does your compassionate nature set you up to be taken advantage of?
- By putting others first, do you find that your own needs go unmet?

If you answered "yes" to most of these questions, then you naturally align most closely with the Water Element. You want to preserve your pacifist nature, but keep it balanced as well. Since your strongest suit is tending to others, make sure your own well is always full. While you naturally put others' needs before your own, understand that if you don't tend to what you need, you may end up empty and depleted. Your nature provides a lot of "outpouring" but not a lot of "filling up." It is essential for you to nurture and protect yourself first, not only so you can stay strong and healthy, but also so you remain available to others as you fulfill your various roles in their lives.

A REAL-LIFE PACIFIST

My Aunt Grace was the second born of eight children on my mother's side. My grandparents had four sons and four daughters. Since she was the first-born daughter, Aunt Grace ranked right up there with my grandmother when it came to taking care of the other children, as well as managing the domestic responsibilities; ensuring that the household ran smoothly. From a very young age, Aunt Grace helped my grandmother cook, bake, clean and take care of the younger ones as they appeared on the scene.

She was about 45 years old when I was born so I always remember Aunt Grace in her adult years. She stood about 5 feet, 5 inches tall – actually the tallest of her sisters – and had a slim figure. Her noticeably high cheek bones were clearly her most prominent facial feature, reminding me of Katherine Hepburn.

She didn't spend a lot of time "prettying herself up" when she went to work – she didn't have to. Her skin was flawless. She had a naturally radiant complexion which, thinking back now, looked a lot like the dewy glow most people nowadays can only get from a bottle costing a small fortune. Aunt Grace may have applied a little powder to her nose and a light stroke of coral colored lipstick, but that was the extent of her morning makeup routine. She would quickly run a brush though her thick, prematurely white hair, and somehow wrap all the ends around one hand. With her other hand, she would hastily slide the bobby pins she held between her teeth upwards, downwards and sideways into her hair that was wrapped around her hand, and invariably create the neatest French twist. In a matter of minutes, and with minimal effort, Aunt Grace looked stunning. She was the perfect representation of her name.

Aunt Grace spent her career as a legal secretary for a small law firm in town. She was essentially responsible for keeping the firm, which consisted of a family of 5 attorneys, plus two young associates, running smoothly. She was the cohesive element that kept it all together. Aunt Grace's work ethic was impeccable. She was smart, thorough, responsible and cared about her work, her employers and their clients.

When I was young, maybe 9 or 10, I would occasionally ride into town with my Aunt MaryRuth to pick up Aunt Grace from work. Whenever I'd go into the office shortly before 5 p.m., Aunt Grace would proudly introduce me to the attorneys. I saw how much they thought of Aunt Grace and how much she respected them. Looking back, I'm not sure if that whole scenario made me want to go to law school or not, but it certainly left a lasting impression on me.

Aunt Grace (the eldest daughter) and Aunt MaryRuth (the youngest daughter) lived with my grandparents in the family home. Aunt Grace never married and had no children, but she was every bit a "second mother" to almost everyone in the family: my mother, my other aunts, my uncles, my father, me and my cousins. Aunt Grace played a prominent role in all of our lives. She left a positive and lasting impression on each of us.

Although my youngest aunt received some help through scholarship money, Aunt Grace essentially put Aunt MaryRuth through college. That was no small feat back then. My mother always remembered in those days Aunt Grace could "stretch a nickel."

In a big family, where everyone still lived in the neighborhood or just down the block, they all still gathered at my grandparents' home for Sunday dinner. Although my parents and I lived an hour away, we were always there after church. I loved those Sunday dinners at my grandparents. Being an only child, I never had the experience of fighting for attention, or competing with a sibling. Those Sunday dinners taught me, however, that brothers and sisters have an entirely different relationship with one another that I will never be privy to. And, surprisingly, they will still have hurt feelings, compete with one another, and disagree like children no matter how old they are.

It was always Aunt Grace who called everyone to let them know that dinner was soon to be on the table. If an in-law couldn't make it for dinner, it was Aunt Grace who always sent a plate of food home for them. It was always Aunt Grace who cooled the flames of a heated argument at the table. It was always Aunt Grace who smoothed over hurt feelings after a family disagreement. And, if someone left in a huff, it was always Aunt Grace who recruited another family member to bring them some leftovers after dinner was over. She was the cohesive force of the family. She calmed things down and kept relationships flowing smoothly.

Aunt Grace always put others first. Never once do I recall Aunt Grace acting selfishly, or putting her own needs before anyone else's. Perhaps that's how she earned the highest compliment you could ever pay anyone when my dad told me "I would trust Grace with my life." Maybe that's also why everyone sought out her sage advice. It was Aunt Grace who my cousin cried to when her husband left her and needed guidance.

In my relationship with Aunt Grace, I was always the one who initiated the words "I love you," and I distinctly remember her response: "Oh, I love *you*, sweetheart," always stressing the "you." Thinking back now, she didn't have to initiate those words "I love you" because she showed it. She always listened intently, offered the most compassionate viewpoint, and always, *always*, came from a place of unconditional love for every one of us. You could just feel her love wash over you. It was nourishing, deep and comforting and you always felt better because of it.

After a decades-long career working at the law firm, I remember Aunt Grace decided to retire so that she could take care of my grandparents. She took care of them with the same unconditional love and respect she showed to everyone. Within a seven-year period, my grandparents and my Aunt MaryRuth passed away, leaving Aunt Grace all alone. And within a short period of time thereafter, Aunt Grace developed Alzheimer's disease. Fortunately, it was this same "at home" care that Aunt Grace provided to my grandparents that we were able to give to Aunt Grace. The family put forth all their efforts to make her life the very best it could be. By that time, many of Aunt Grace's siblings had passed on, but the in-laws who still lived in the neighborhood graciously rallied to help Aunt Grace by staying with her and cooking for her to make her life pleasant and safe. Although she became confused easily, Aunt Grace's compassionate nature was still evident.

I remember one instance when Aunt Grace, then about 90 years old, was grilling my mother, then about 82 years old, with questions, insisting to know: "Where is your mother? Is she with you? Are you going to go pick her up? Is she coming back? Is she waiting for you?" After about 5 solid minutes of this unrelenting questioning, and several unsuccessful attempts are "re-directing" Aunt Grace's attention, my mother had had all she could take and, with exasperation, forcefully exclaimed: "My mother died!" Aunt Grace recoiled and with the most compassionate look and in an effort to comfort my mother said "Oh, I'm so *sorry!*" My mother, however, unwisely decided to add: "My mother was *your* mother!" which just threw more unnecessary information into an already trying conversation and, of course, elicited a very confused look from Aunt Grace.

Although her condition progressively eroded her memory, her speech, and her ability to reason, I still witnessed the strength of Aunt Grace's love emanate from her more strongly than ever before. Whenever I entered the room Aunt Grace's eyes would fixate on me. She didn't have to speak because I knew what she was conveying albeit on a different level. I still felt that familiar, unconditional love from her. And this makes sense to me – that kind of love transcends mind and speech and breaks through every kind of barrier.

A few years after Aunt Grace passed away, I had a memorable encounter during a ski weekend with some friends. After dinner one evening, I noticed a man sitting at a table not far from where we were walking out. I knew I had seen him throughout the years, and I knew it was related to my work, but I couldn't immediately place him. It finally dawned on me that he was one of the young attorneys Aunt Grace used to work for. I figured he would never remember who I was, but to honor Aunt Grace, I went up to re-acquaint myself with him. Before I could complete the sentence "Patrick, I'm sure you don't remember . . ." he immediately said "Yes I do know who you are. You're Grace's niece!" From our brief conversation, it was obvious that Aunt Grace left a lasting impression and her spirit was still bringing people closer together.

MORE ABOUT THE WATER ELEMENT

The Water Element is synonymous with the growth, development and nourishment of our body. On an emotional level, the Water Element represents fluidity and cohesion in our life. It provides for a calming demeanor, a compassionate nature, and an ability and desire to get along well with others. The Water Element provides us with the temperament to keep relationships and tasks running smoothly.

WATER AS GROWTH

Perhaps our first introduction to the Water Element was the amniotic fluid that surrounded us in our mother's womb. Among other things, its high nutrient content helped to develop our musculoskeletal system, our lungs and our digestive system.[29]

In plants, water is absorbed through their root system, travels up their stem and is distributed throughout the entire plant through its capillary-like xylem vessels. Water regulates the plant's temperature and moisture levels for its successful maturity. Water is the source of life and the most basic nourishment for the body. To put it simply, as water begins to flow, life grows.

WATER AS CLEANSING

Water is a powerful cleansing agent. We use it daily to shower or wash our bodies and clean our homes, offices, cars, and our belongings.

Water is also known as "the universal solvent."[30] In light of its chemical composition, water is attracted to numerous types of molecules — some potentially harmful — and can readily dissolve them, perhaps better than any other liquid can. For example, water is essential to proper kidney functioning. It effectively dissolves and ushers out the toxins our kidneys have filtered from the food and drinks we have consumed. On a symbolic level, the act of baptism in water represents cleansing of our sins and washing them away.

WATER AS COOLING

Water is the antidote to heat. Consider its role in the design of an automobile. In order to keep the engine from overheating, water is continuously distributed to the engine, via passages in the engine block and cylinder heads. After the water flows through those passages and picks up the heat from the engine, it then circulates back into the radiator where a steady stream of air entering through the grill keeps it cool. After it is cooled, the water recirculates back to the engine once again to absorb more heat.

WATER AS CALMING

The calming nature of water certainly creates an attractive option whenever people are planning the birth of their children. If they choose to only labor in water – water immersion – the process may be less stressful for the mother. If they choose to stay in the water for the actual delivery – water birth – the idea is that the water creates an external environment for the baby that's similar to the environment it has been use to in mother's womb. Many view water birth as a more gentle way of bringing a baby into the world. Either way, it's water's very nature and its ability to calm the entire process for all involved that make it so desirable.[31]

WATER AS PROTECTION

The first representation of the protective nature of the Water Element we experienced was the amniotic fluid that enveloped each of us as babies in our mother's womb. It made it easier for us to move around and functioned as an ideal "shock-absorbing system" as it cushioned us against any bumps or blows to our mother's abdomen.[32]

Out of the womb, the Water Element remains an integral part of protecting and regulating the internal balance of our body. Our body is composed of approximately 70% water; our brain up to 85% water; and our blood up to 80% water.[33]

In order to remain healthy and maintain homeostasis, our body tells us when we need more water by triggering us to feel thirsty. While our body can survive weeks without solid food, it can survive only a matter of days without water.

WATER AS BEAUTY

If you want to be mesmerized by the sheer power and beauty of the Water Element, just talk to a surfer. No doubt many will tell you that a long ride "inside the tube" (the hollow of a huge, crashing wave) is the equivalent of finding surfing's Holy Grail. When you listen to surfers like Gerry Lopez and others talk about their surfing adventures it's like listening to someone relate a spiritual experience, as they speak in terms of "oneness," "rapture," "awe" and even "seeing God"[34]

. . . And as Destruction

Now think about the huge destructive force of a Tsunami which is created by a series of ocean waves that sends surges of water – sometimes reaching a height of over 100 feet – crashing onto land.

Tsunami waves are caused by undersea earthquakes, undersea landslides, or undersea volcanic eruptions. They can race with tremendous speed, around 500 mph. While they slow down as they approach the shoreline, they simultaneously increase in energy and height.[35]

Water is heavy, and although it is fluid, with increased speed and energy, it becomes like a moving solid wall. Everything and everyone in its path are helpless. The overwhelming experience of a deluge of water results in submersion, smothering, overpowering and suffocation.

WATER IN THE BODY

Some of the major roles the Water Element plays in our physiology are: "regulator," "nourisher" and "protector."

Perhaps the most recognizable form of water we can see in the body is the salivary fluid in our mouth. Saliva keeps the mouth moist when we eat. Our taste buds are triggered only when water or saliva is present. Simply put: No water, no taste. Saliva contains the enzyme ptyalin, which aids in the initial stages of digesting starch in the food we consume, and the chemical lysozyme, which protects the mouth from infection.[36]

The Water Element also appears within the mucosal lining of our stomach. Our stomach lining produces a fluid of sorts that helps break down food and aid in our digestion. This fluid protects the stomach lining as well from excessive heat or dryness, and from the effects of hydrochloric acid and other acidic gastric enzymes.

We find a small, but integral, amount of the Water Element in our thoracic cavity. We refer to it as pleural fluid, which lubricates the pleura around the lungs so they can glide over each other as we breathe.

Pericardial fluid, another example of the Water Element, reduces the friction within the pericardium by lubricating the epicardial surface, and allowing the membranes to glide over each other with each heartbeat.

Cerebrospinal fluid is yet another example of the Water Element in our body. This fluid protects the brain and spinal cord from trauma, it bathes the brain and spine in nutrients, and it removes waste products from cerebral metabolism. This fluid also stabilizes the flow of neurological impulses.[37]

Whether it is hinging joints of the knees, elbows and fingers, gliding joints of the spine, wrists and tarsal bones of the feet, or ball and socket joints of the hips and shoulders, synovial fluid is yet another example of the Water Element in our body. This fluid nourishes and lubricates the cartilage and bones inside the joint capsules. In most cases synovial fluid is essential to help prevent the wear and tear of our joints.[38]

When the Water Element is in proper balance in the body, our systems are in good working order and running smoothly. There are no glitches in our systems' functioning. The skin is also clear and smooth.

When the Water Element in the body increases, however, you're going to experience some issues. Excess water may begin with heaviness in the abdomen and develop into obesity. Excess fluid can appear as asthma, bronchitis, or pleurisy. You may also see swollen joints as fluid accumulates at those sites. "Damp conditions," like edema, congestion, phlegm in the throat, catarrh (excessive buildup or discharge of mucous in the nose and throat), water retention, and sinus or yeast infections may develop in the body from excess fluid accumulation.

When the Water Element is insufficient in the body, it will likely manifest in the areas mentioned above but in a dry or inflammatory way: We may see receding gums in the mouth, gastritis in the stomach, memory loss in the brain or rheumatoid arthritis in the joints. We experience dehydration as our cells begin to dry out. We may develop dry mucous membranes, dry skin, dry eyes and dry lips, weight loss, a noticeable decrease in urination and perspiration, and the formation of dry, hard stools.

WATER IN THE MIND

The Water Element in the mind manifests as clarity of thought, compassion, and the desire to bond with others. We want to ensure that the Water Element remains calm and does not turn into a deluge.

If the Water Element in the mind increases, it – and you – can be overwhelming. Calm waters can turn into a flood and spread into every nook and cranny.

You may pour out your compassionate nature to others to provide advice and protection even when it's not asked for or desired. Excess water in the mind has the power to drown and to suffocate.

On the other hand, your compassion for others may leave you vulnerable. You give willingly but perhaps can't see how others may take advantage of such generosity.

If the Water Element in the mind decreases, it's similar to when your body becomes dehydrated: you become sluggish. A once content demeanor can turn into a feeling of apathy.

When in balance, the Water Element promotes a happy and content personality and a calming nature with an inclination to comfort and protect.

THE ACTION PLAN FOR THE PACIFIST

While compassion for others is one of your most prized qualities, you'll want to establish emotional boundaries so your good nature doesn't keep "flowing out" thereby tempting others to take advantage of you. Although you feel compelled to protect others from physical and emotional harm, learn when to step back so you don't smother or drowned the people you're trying to protect. When asked, give your best advice to others, with their best interests in mind, but allow them to choose what they want to do with it.

Although you typically put others' needs first, don't ignore your own needs. You must nurture yourself just like you nurture others. It's second nature for you to take care of other people, but if you don't nurture and care for yourself, you're at risk to become depleted, both physically and emotionally.

You want to maintain your easygoing, fluid nature, but don't let your calm attitude become awash with sluggishness or complacency.

TECHNIQUES FOR BRINGING THE PACIFIST BACK TO BALANCE

THINKING: When the Pacifist becomes imbalanced it takes some extra effort to "right the ship." Remember, your natural element is associated with water and that means smooth sailing when skies are clear but the danger of capsizing from encountering collisions or towering waves. Maybe you're listing to the right when you're feeling you're being taken advantage of in light of your calm and accommodating nature. Or perhaps you're listing to the left when you're feeling apathetic by others under-appreciating your efforts. Either way, water can carry a lot of weight, so you don't want to list too far or for too long.

Remember, a ship lists because it is either damaged or improperly loaded. Maybe your perception is that you're not receiving what you're giving out. Or perhaps you have a tendency to over-extend yourself with others and over-commit your time and energy, eventually to your own undoing. If so, your generally buoyant nature is becoming weighed down. It's your feelings of heaviness and listing that we want to correct. Let's work on properly loading your mindset so you can come up for air and re-chart your course.

Begin by clarifying and bolstering your outlook, then create healthy boundaries.

PRACTICE GRATITUDE: The first step in bringing any listing ship back to an upright position is to re-arrange your cargo so it is more balanced. Granted, we all carry a lot of cargo, but when we feel overwhelmed or taken advantage of, or when nothing looks right, take a more objective approach and examine what you have. Yes, examine what you have in front of you. Take the time to look around and see what is working for you and to appreciate all the things you're grateful for.

It's a process called Practicing Gratitude. It provides reflection, a sense of understanding and appreciation. Ultimately it brings you back to the "bigger picture" and reveals the cohesion in your life's journey. It brings an "order" to your life that you can't see unless you step out of the fray and begin to observe.

Gratitude for what you already have automatically brings your focus to the present moment. It puts you in a positive mindset. It helps you to identify the goodness in your life. It helps you to see that you have received support from others, or from a Higher Power.

Gratitude causes you to appreciate the value of something in your life and not take it for granted. You're not looking elsewhere for good things, rather you're seeing good things in your life right now.[39]

When you contemplate your gifts in life, you will see that life has moved in your favor more times than you realize.

Only you can list the things you're grateful for and I urge you to do so.

Begin with today and what you have done, who you've spoken with, where you've gone and who you've seen. Dig deep. Isolate moments, thoughts, and conversations. Contemplate what has gone well today and why you're grateful it has.

Scroll through the people, places, and circumstances in your life that bring a smile to your face. Call to mind family members, friends, or pets. Or think about those times you knew you were guided and protected by a Higher Power. Think about people and circumstances that make you feel safe or make your life easier in any way. Be grateful for your health and for your senses of sight, hearing, taste, touch and smell. Be grateful for your ability to learn, inspirations you receive, your good mind, and your ability to change your mind.

Your mind is the most powerful tool you have. It determines whether you will have smooth sailing or constantly struggle with choppy waters. Always remember that your thoughts direct your energy. Your perspective is one of the keys to living a happy life. Be grateful for your ability to adopt a healthy perspective throughout your life and your ability to always choose to see the glass as half full.

Be grateful for your ability to choose a goal and to go after it. Be grateful that you can choose what you want in your life, your ability to visualize it and create it the best way you know how. Remember that whatever you focus your attention on will grow.

Be grateful that you can always take a step back and wisely choose your reaction. It can save you and others a lot of heartache and upset.

There is always something for you to be grateful for. When you call to mind even one thing and contemplate just how fortunate you are, you will attract into your life more things to be grateful for.

DEVELOP A POSITIVE MINDSET WITH DAILY AFFIRMATIONS: In your effort to get back on-course, your best navigation tool is a positive mindset. As you constantly surround yourself with positive thoughts you begin to view your world and the people in it with a much more positive light. And as you continue to clarify your perspective, a positive mindset will have you sailing smoothly in no time flat.

One of the best ways to cultivate a positive mindset is to use positive affirmations. People use them primarily to shift their attitudes about themselves. Remember, whenever you're dealing with other people, don't make your mental outlook, your well-being, or your happiness dependent on other people's reactions or opinions. Don't think that you'll be sailing smoothly as soon as other people start to appreciate you, or as soon as they stop taking advantage of you, or as soon as they realize that their actions are taking a toll on you. They won't. You must understand that it's entirely up to you to build and bolster your own outlook and perspective. You're the only one who has the power to control your behavior and your reactions to situations. Do not give up your power to someone else. Cultivate and maintain your own power.

Positive affirmations focus on you and the state you want to be in. They only work on you, not on others. They are a great way to focus on your own circumstances, goals, behavior and desired outcomes.

I think the best way to "cook up" a great positive affirmation is to follow a great recipe:

TITLE: Positive Affirmation

YIELDS: Peace of Mind, Happiness and a Healthy Perspective

SERVES: 1 (well into the future)

INGREDIENTS: Positive words only (no "don't", "can't" or "won't")

RELEVANT INTENTION: Specifically address what you want to accomplish in this situation. Add an emotional word to charge your feeling about the affirmation (optional, but highly recommended!)

PREPARATION METHOD: Declare what you want to be true about yourself or about your life. Earnestly bring to mind what you want to accomplish – not in terms of "I might" or "I could." Be firm in your intention. Formulate a statement which clearly conveys the truth you want to set forth. Phrase your statement in the present tense as if stating a fact. Use words like "am" and "do," not "I will" or "I used to." Combine the positive words in the present tense to convey a statement about your intention. Here are some examples of positive affirmations that you may want to start with:

I provide my time and energy in relationships to the extent they are necessary.
I respect my own time and energy.
I feel confident in my relationships.
I am positively energized by my relationships.

TIP: The way you phrase your statement is crucial because your brain communicates in the present tense; not in the future or the past. Your brain reacts to your thoughts in the present moment, as though you are experiencing your thoughts right now. Your brain is looking for a command. Positive affirmations are spoken as statements of fact and truth. They speak the language of the brain.

VARIATIONS: Write out your positive affirmation on a piece of paper. Set up a routine to repeat your affirmation throughout the day. Repeating your positive affirmation(s) for at least 5 minutes, 3 times per day will yield optimal results because your brain strengthens connections every time you think, feel and do.

SETTING PHYSICAL AND EMOTIONAL BOUNDARIES: What to do when others want more from us: Make sure not to over-extend yourself more than is physically possible. Make sure you don't commit yourself to be somewhere or to help someone if that means "overbooking" your own schedule or cutting someone else short. Do not physically drain yourself. You know when you're absolutely needed somewhere. You know when it's appropriate to juggle your time and activities. The danger comes when you don't realize that you're constantly juggling and short-changing yourself and those who are truly in need of your help. Really evaluate where you want to focus your energy and your efforts.

Make sure not to over-extend yourself emotionally, or worse, take on other people's problems. Both will exhaust you. Keep in mind that each one of us has the means to solve our own problems, big or small. Sometimes it just takes someone else's keen perspective and thoughtful advice to reveal our tools and ingenuity to do so. Over-extending yourself emotionally or taking on someone else's problems doesn't lessen the load or relieve the burden for that person. It simply spreads around the heaviness and worry. Give people your best advice and trust in their capabilities to do what they think is best.

What to do when we want to give more to others than they ask for: You can give people your best advice, and you can warn them of dangers along the way. And you can even plot out a course of action for them. But remember, it is ultimately their choice to follow your advice or not. Everyone has their own journey to travel. It is their own learning experience. To do otherwise would deprive them of the lessons they came here to learn. Give them your best, but allow them to choose.

FEELING: Rein in your day a bit more as you really pay attention to where and how you're expending your energy. Take stock of where you're being depleted and where you can add more enjoyment into your life.

TAKE STOCK OF YOUR DAY : Create an hourly schedule of your day and write down everything you do each hour of the day. Study it and see where your energy is seeping away and exhausting you. Identify in your day what you are doing that provides you with energy and what you are doing that robs your energy.

CREATE A PLAN: Build a plan for each day to maximize your energy intake and minimize your energy drains and non-productivity. Set time limits and time frames for yourself and others. Set goals and see them to completion. Shore up any loose ends. Factor in and prioritize your own well-being for sleeping, eating, working and leisure. Within your workday, establish specific times to manage emails and to make or return phone calls.

REDUCE MULTI-TASKING: Minimize multi-tasking – it's not all that it's cracked up to be! We often find ourselves doing more than one thing at a time. We think we're accomplishing tasks, but we're actually draining ourselves. Rarely are we turning out anything of quality. If we're enjoying a great conversation, only to be interrupted by the insistent ring of our cell phone, what have we really gained? We're spreading ourselves very thin and it's unfair to those we're spending time with. We may think it's a real accomplishment to get a lot of things completed in a short amount of time, but the real challenge comes when we're called upon to be fully present. The real gift is to give our undivided attention to the task, or person, at hand for as long as necessary. Everyone involved is better for it.

EATING: To keep the Water Element balanced in the body, you want to encourage a flow, yet prevent a deluge. Pay particular attention to the energies of the foods you eat – do they increase or decrease the bulk or the moisture level in your body? Also take into consideration various cooking methods and the influence they have on the moistness or dryness of your body.

THE QUALITIES OF SWEET AND SALTY FOODS – PACIFISTS SHOULD PROCEED WITH CAUTION AND IN MODERATION: Take the time to pay attention to the energies of the foods you eat and their effect on the Water Element. For example, foods with an energetically "sweet" taste – most whole grains, cooked root vegetables, sugary foods, sweet fruits like bananas or dates, dairy, and honey – are nourishing, but they are quite heavy by nature, and have a tendency to increase bulk in our body.

Foods with an energetically "salty" taste – any kind of salt, sea vegetables, salted snacks – are lubricating when consumed in moderation, but salty foods will create excess moisture in the body over time because they attract water.

Being naturally aligned with the Water Element, the Pacifist will likely already have enough bulk and moisture in their body without the need to add more. Make sure not to over-emphasize sweet and salty foods in your diet. If you do consume them, do so in moderation.

THE BENEFITS OF ASTRINGENT FOODS TO BALANCE THE PACIFIST: Astringent foods are an integral part of bringing the Pacifist back into balance. Although they may make your mouth pucker when you eat them, astringent foods have a contracting and drying quality as they naturally absorb excess water and tighten tissues. These foods will address water retention, or congestion, to help the Pacifist regain equilibrium. Other benefits of consuming astringent foods are that they assist in stopping bleeding, tighten tissues, dry fat, and heal skin wounds, ulcers and mucous membranes. They also have antibiotic and antibacterial qualities.

Foods like beans and lentils; fruits like cranberries, pomegranates and pears; and vegetables like green beans, cabbage and peas are great choices. Remember, astringent foods work to "constrict" excess water, and are perfect for the Pacifist to counterbalance their natural tendency to accumulate water.

INCORPORATE DRY COOKING METHODS: While the Pacifist naturally has ample moisture in their body, the kind of cooking methods to employ should be the drier ones. If you're trying to rebalance a physiology that is "damp" – one that shows signs of sinus congestion, yeast infection, bloating, or asthma – Pacifists should employ drier cooking methods rather than adding more water to an already overly-saturated body. Here are some recommended cooking techniques that will work best to bring Pacifists back to equilibrium:

BAKING: This process uses prolonged dry heat; liquids evaporate during this process
BROILING: applying dry heat to food typically from above
GRILLING: applying dry heat to food typically from below

If, however, you find yourself in need of more water in your body, remember that moist cooking methods like steaming, boiling or poaching will add water to the cooking process and will bring more moisture to your tissues. They are good choices if you find yourself unnecessarily drying out.

The Rock

DOES THE ROCK SOUND LIKE YOU?
It's the Rock who will help others weather the storms in life. It seems like their broad shoulders can take on the weight of the world—and they still won't complain. The Rock's loyalty to family and friends is strong and may even outlast others' own belief in themselves. They remain steadfast in their ideas and convictions and will encourage others to do the same. The Rock is a true friend and will never leave anyone's side, especially when they're needed.

ATTRIBUTES:
- Do you have stamina and endurance in mental and physical pursuits?
- Do you commit yourself fully in personal and professional relationships?
- Do you find that your thoughts or advice to others is more on the practical side?
- Can you remain true to your convictions when others present opposing views?
- Are you satisfied if someone else takes the lead in a project?

YET, PERHAPS:
- Do you become attached to old methods and, therefore, resistant to change?
- Do you find yourself often inflexible in your perspective?
- Can you become stuck in a cycle of thinking that's hard to release from?

If you answered "yes" to most of these questions, then you naturally align most closely with the Earth Element. You want to maintain your sturdy nature, but keep it balanced as well. Preserving your unmatched qualities of commitment and loyalty is paramount, but balance them with a sense of space, lightness and reason. Of course, you don't want to be disappointed if something doesn't work out, but if things don't go the way you expected them to go, don't dig your heels in and hold onto a position that doesn't serve you. Your undying loyalty to people and positions can hold you back when you must make a decision otherwise. Keep it light, give it space and stay active.

A REAL-LIFE ROCK

Jen is a great friend who I met when we were freshmen in college. We lived in the same dormitory building, but she lived on the 3rd floor and I lived on the 1st floor. Our paths crisscrossed throughout our freshman and sophomore years (I spent my junior year studying abroad), but I really got to know her well when I returned for our senior year.

Jen was from a small town in Western Pennsylvania where her family owned a well-known and hugely successful lumber yard business. You never would have learned of the success of her family's business from Jen herself. She was not one to brag, nor to coast on the success of her family. Jen remained firmly rooted in her belief that she would stand on her own two feet and earn her own ticket through life.

Perhaps it was the influence of growing up in a family owned business that caused Jen to follow a very practical course of study by majoring in Economics. Or maybe it was a more practical "cover up" for her real interest in Comparative Religions, which was her minor.

Jen had two older brothers and from what I remember of their family dynamic, each brother's relationship with their parents was strained at best. It became clear, that from an early age, Jen tried to manage relationships she wasn't even involved in.

Jen wasn't a "flashy" dresser in college. She wore clothes that were stylish and tasteful yet understated. Jen was in a constant struggle with her weight, but her winning personality outshone any perceived challenge she may have had. Jen was pretty, she was friendly, and she was down to earth.

Our college years spanned the early 1980's which celebrated "big hair" and bold makeup. Jen had the prettiest big blue eyes and apparently the steadiest hand and perfect touch to apply one stroke of liquid navy eyeliner (lining inner and outer, upper and lower lash lines) to accentuate them and she finished the look with just a light dusting of two-toned blue eyeshadow. While the popular "dramatic" look emphasized more of a raccoon eye, Jen's make-up was toned-down and flawless.

Kristine, Yvonne, Jen and I enjoyed our college years together. Our personalities were quite different, but we all agreed that Jen was the most grounded. Although occasionally she went out to parties, she was more of a homebody, albeit a "dorm room homebody." It wasn't her style to boast about anything she did, but instead she preferred to shine the spotlight on someone else.

Jen's best quality by far was her ability to make those around her feel comfortable. Our small group of friends loved to hang out together and always ended up at Jen's dorm room to kick back and relax. I remember she always added that extra touch to our gatherings by brewing a pot of flavored coffee which was the perfect accompaniment as we laughed, talked about our plans for the future, and took our turns blowing off steam.

Whether we complained about studying, classmates, or professors; sought advice about clothes, makeup, or hair styles; or tossed around ideas about our future, it was always Jen who consistently came up with the most practical advice and workable solutions.

I remember an endearing characteristic that Jen had whenever she was relaying a story to us. She spoke of the other people who were involved by first name only, as if we were supposed to already know exactly who they were. At first it drove me crazy – not only did I have to piece together the storyline; I didn't even know who the characters were! And then it dawned on me, she presumed that since the other people were either friends or family of hers, they must automatically be friends of ours. At first, I couldn't understand her manner of talking, but as time went on, I considered it to be a form of closeness.

Jen worked hard throughout college and studied earnestly. That's how she approached her life; with determination and a steady movement forward. Campus was only a short distance from downtown Meadville, and I remember Jen, Kristine and I would often walk back and forth to town. Occasionally, when we became involved in a really good conversation, Kristine and I would lag behind chatting away, and Jen would plod along ahead – sure and steady. In a feeble effort to get Jen to wait up for us "slackers," we shouted out to her: "Hey, slow down, there's a speed limit on this street!"

When her father passed away, the task of anchoring the family fell to Jen. It was Jen who bore the weight of keeping some semblance of connection between her brothers and their mother. While those relationships remained strained, Jen provided the necessary support to at least maintain the status quo. While they likely weren't going to improve, Jen still had the ability and the right touch to prevent those relationships from completely unraveling. She was unfailingly loyal to her mother as she willingly stepped into the role of her mom's emotional pillar.

It was surprising to me the few occasions that Jen let out any inkling of emotional overload from her family situation, as that wasn't her style. You could tell there was much more raw emotion behind the few cryptic comments that seeped past her "business as usual" voice. At times I felt as if she was about to explode, but she kept her emotions together as she continued to take on more of the same and accumulate them almost as if she were stuffing them into a bottomless vessel.

In our senior year, Jen began dating a guy in our graduating class. I didn't know him, but she was absolutely crazy about him. From what I understood they went out a couple of times. He decided to move on, but she didn't. Although their dating life ended, his memory continued on in her head. She just couldn't get over him. She kept obsessing about him and their last conversation, as she kept asking the same questions over and over: Why? What was he really saying? Did he actually mean that? Throughout our senior year, we were still hearing her replay these questions over and over again.

Several years after graduation Kristine, Yvonne, Jen and I got together again at a downtown Pittsburgh restaurant. We talked about our lives, our jobs, our new endeavors, our new friends, our new loves, but the same conversation still played in Jen's head. She didn't leave this guy's memory in college. She took it with her beyond graduation. He continued to live in her mind. Same guy. Same obsession. Same stories. Same questions. Same inability to let go of her notion that they were supposed to be together. It was troubling to see someone so grounded, practical, and supportive of others obsess over this man. It was clear that she was attached to her drama and had no plans of letting it go.

After years of successfully working in retail in the central Mid-West, Jen returned back to her hometown, moved in with her mother, and took the next logical career step and opened her own business. Shortly after its grand opening, I made a point to drive out to visit with her and see her newest endeavor.

Two houses were situated on the property her family owned. She and her mother lived in one of the houses, and Jen renovated the other house from a typical 1950's ranch style into the most beautiful, charming craft store I ever saw. She put in French doors where the garage door used to be which added an elegant flair and created the most welcoming feeling as you walked in. She kept the rooms of the house as they were intended to be (kitchen, bathroom, bedrooms, living room) but she decorated them in an authentic early American style.

The scent of candles permeated the air and you couldn't help but linger and wander through the house eagerly taking in all the sights and scents. One room just flowed into the next. Her eye for detail was amazing. She took every nook and cranny into consideration. There wasn't anywhere your eyes landed that had been overlooked or glossed over. I was mesmerized, yet knowing Jen, not surprised by the thoughtfulness, the thoroughness, and comfort she had created.

I remember walking into the kitchen and the jolt of reality when I saw price tags on the jars of jelly, subtly reminding me that this was, in fact, a business endeavor. I decided to buy a jar of red pepper jelly but the payment for it seemed much less valuable than the experience her shoppe left with me. A few years later, Jen decided to add furniture to her inventory, which only made her store and her business even more successful.

Jen is the kind of friend everyone should have – solid and dependable. Everyone who knows Jen is better off for having her in their life.

MORE ABOUT THE EARTH ELEMENT

Earth is the densest of all five Elements. It represents the solid state of matter and it promotes the energies of accumulation and construction. The Earth Element is the source of the raw materials our physical structure utilizes in order to form and maintain its strength. Food remains the primary means through which the Earth Element enters our body. Once we have reached our full structural potential, the Earth Element still provides us with the raw materials we use to rejuvenate our physical form.

EARTH AS PRIMARILY SOLID

The Earth's crust is the outermost shell of our planet and the layer upon which we live. The crust's surface has cooled and hardened. To give you an idea of its depth, the Earth's crust underlies the oceans' floors – in those circumstances the crust is composed of volcanic, or basalt, rock – and it underlies the continents – in those circumstances the crust is composed of granite.[40]

Below the covering of the Earth's crust lies another layer called the Mantle which has a solid/plastic consistency. The top and bottom of the Earth's Mantle are solid, but the center of the mantle consists of a more thick, sticky substance somewhere between a solid and a liquid. Its composition of immensely hot, dense rock gives the center of the earth's Mantle its highly viscous qualities.

Beneath the Earth's Mantle lies the Outer Core which is composed of melted nickel and iron. The Outer Core is so hot that the metals are in a liquid state. The Earth's Inner Core, however, is composed of a solid iron-nickel alloy.[41]

EARTH AS STABLE

To me, those massive, rugged mountains of the Scottish Highlands towering over the lush green valleys below them is one of the most dramatic sights on earth for viewing actual earth. Those immense mountains perfectly showcase the strength and stability of the Earth Element.

It's this same stability I vividly remember when I climbed to the top of Iseler Mountain in the Alps. I spent my junior year of college studying in Germany. Before the official start of the academic year in October, my classmates and I traveled to the small Bavarian town of Oberjoch where we prepared for the entrance examination to the University of Tübingen. We spent two weeks in a beautiful chalet nestled in the mountains where we attended classes every morning to study grammar, vocabulary, reading comprehension, writing, and conversation. Our afternoons were also full as we enjoyed structured free time.

One beautiful warm, sunny afternoon we were guided on a hike to the top of Iseler Mountain. I thought we were just taking an easy "nature walk" and didn't really have any idea we were going to the summit of a mountain. As we continued to ascend, I remained focused to make sure that my feet were firmly planted on the ground each step of the way. I wasn't a mountain climber, or even a hiker, but I knew that the stability I felt as I took each step would support me with all the help I needed. With that plan as my "road map," I confidently reached the summit and was greeted by its gorgeous view.

EARTH AS HEAVY AND THICK

Whether it's holding a clump of earth in the palm of their hand or stomping on a shovel and turning up a patch of ground, farmers and gardeners in particular can tell your first-hand about the weight, the density and the feel of earth.

My first experience with gardening was in the summer of 2006 when I decided to replicate a "square foot garden" at home from a seminar I attended. Staying as true to the directions as possible, we built a wooden box, filled it with beautiful rich, dark, organic soil, and divided it with string into twelve equal squares, each one measuring one foot by one foot. In each square, we planted different organic vegetables: radishes in one, leaf lettuce in another, carrots in another, and kohlrabi in yet another. As each square was harvested, we planted something different in its place. This organic square-foot garden project was the first time I remember sinking my hands into soft, black soil, and really paying attention to the heavy, thick, nutrient-laden earth and contemplating the integral role it plays in the healthy formation of our food.

EARTH AS STRUCTURE AND FORM

Building with earth is a technique that has been around for thousands of years. When earth is used as a building material, it yields very practical results: It regulates indoor temperatures, insulates against heat and cold, and acts as a natural humidifier, when dry. Earthen buildings are extremely strong and durable.

We can clearly see the beauty and practicality of earthen construction on display as we scroll through history and study various locations across the globe. Whether it was the Walls of Jericho, the Cob Homes of Great Britain, the Rammed Earth techniques seen in The Great Wall of China, or the more familiar images of the Adobe mud bricks of the Southwestern United States, using earth to build structures optimizes their sturdy and lasting qualities.

EARTH IN COLLAPSE AND DISINTEGRATION

When the Earth is provoked to move, it can be disastrous especially because of its heavy and dense qualities. Whenever a large mass of earth (rock, soil or debris) moves down a slope under the influence of gravity it not only upends what it is supporting, but it travels with such velocity and momentum in its downward movement that it can demolish buildings, destroy infrastructure, crush bridges and highways, and cause tremendous damage to the environment.

In May of 1980 you may remember the 5.1 magnitude earthquake which triggered the volcanic eruption of Mount St. Helens in Washington state. The largest landslide in U.S. history ensued. The earth and debris from the landslide travelled 14 miles and destroyed everything in its path, including 9 highway bridges. Statistics indicate that the amount of debris from this landslide could have filled 250 million dump trucks.[42]

EARTH IN THE BODY

The Earth Element has a particular affinity for our muscle tissue, for the solid structural component of our bones, and for our adipose fat tissue, which stores energy in the form of fat, as well as cushions and insulates the body. These tissues create a healthy "Earth Element" in our body and, in turn, they are dependent upon receiving a healthy "Earth Element" from our body to remain intact and functioning well.

Clearly, the Earth is rich in minerals. It's these minerals that feed the parts of our body associated with the Earth Element, like our bones and muscles. For example, calcium, boron, copper, iron, and zinc, among other minerals, are integral for bone health.[43] Proper functioning of our muscles requires minerals like calcium, magnesium, potassium and phosphorus.

The Earth Element also creates a "thickening" of structures in our body. We received our first introduction to the Earth Element in our mother's womb through the foods she ate. Those nutrients were responsible for the initial formation and construction of our skeletal system. They were the raw materials that "built" our growing and developing body; providing us with form, structure and density. The Earth Element, through food, continues to provide the raw materials for developing our strength, stamina and endurance.

When the Earth Element increases in our body, primarily through excess eating and not enough physical activity, our body has an overabundance of "raw materials" it typically uses for building new tissues. Where do we store these excess "raw materials" which we have consumed but haven't yet converted into new structures? We store them in the other tissue of our body that has an affinity for the Earth Element – our fat tissue. Consequently, our fat tissue increases in size and becomes larger, thicker and denser.

When the Earth Element is deficient in our body, we don't have the raw materials to maintain or build new structure. We will likely see weakness in our bones, reduced muscle mass, and a decrease in our body fat.

EARTH IN THE MIND

The Earth Element in our mind manifests as the integrity of a strong belief in your own ideas, decisions and values. It is what allows you to firmly stand up for yourself in the world.

In excess, the Earth Element in the mind creates a host of challenging issues. The Earth Element by its very nature is heavy and thick. In the mind, excess Earth will weigh you down. You may become attached to patterns and ways of doing things and approaching situations. It can become hard for you to move or shift directions. Although the Earth Element is naturally grounding, without the motivation to keep moving you may find yourself stuck in old and outdated circumstances, thought patterns and perspectives. In fact, you could actually grind deeper into your old grooves.

The Earth Element has a natural tendency to accumulate. You may find yourself allowing your emotions to stay bottled up inside remaining unreleased and unexpressed. You may not be inclined to share them with anyone.

When the Earth Element is deficient in us, we become weak in the face of adversity. We lack the steadfastness necessary to weather the storm, or to stand strong in our own beliefs. Our convictions will waver as we become susceptible to the will of others.

When the Earth Element is in balance in the mind, it naturally lends itself to a grounded, stable and dependable personality, someone who is aptly described as being "down to earth." You remain a loyal friend or family member and have solid footing and a solid commitment to your relationships.

THE ACTION PLAN FOR THE ROCK

While loyalty is your strong suit, you want to allow some flexibility to change your mind when circumstances warrant a new perspective. Truly believing in someone or something is one of your best traits but allow yourself to change your mind when necessary.

While you are grounded, don't dig yourself into your position so deeply that you can't acknowledge a new way of thinking that may show you a better way.

While you commit to relationships and tasks with your whole being, don't grasp them with an iron fist. Leave breathing room for everyone involved and don't become so attached to an expected outcome.

You have great physical stamina and endurance and can keep grinding away at the same thing for a long time, but don't keep grinding yourself into the same old grooves. Make it a point to add lightness and variety to your routine with foods and activities that are stimulating and motivating.

TECHNIQUES FOR BRINGING THE ROCK BACK INTO BALANCE:

THINKING: The Rock, perhaps more so than the other archetypes, has the tendency to become set in his or her ways so much so that they can turn their own daily routine into an unyielding pattern of drudgery. The Rock can easily become attached to a certain way of doing things – the status quo – and they find change very difficult to tolerate, let alone to initiate. To guard against becoming weighed down by a limited and limiting perspective, the Rock has to take action and breathe new life into their old ways.

VARY YOUR DAILY ROUTINE - DO DIFFERENT THINGS AND DO THINGS DIFFERENTLY: Break up the monotony with change. Take a different route to work. Watch a different kind of show on television. If you're used to watching television sit-coms, try a documentary that sounds interesting to you. Seek out different company and hear what they have to say. Cook a new dish that you've never tried before.

Infuse your taste buds with a different kind of food for a change, if only for one meal. If you don't cook, head out to a restaurant that serves a different kind of fare than you're used to. Introduce your sense of smell to a new scent that will warm you and invigorate you. Burn a stick of incense or diffuse essential oils in your home. Especially good scents for the Rock are warm aromas with spicier overtones like eucalyptus or clove. Basil, or small amounts of frankincense work nicely too. To enhance your sense of touch, try doing a self-massage with warm sesame oil. Applying oil to the skin enhances its health and your sense of touch. Just peer out from under your tired, old routines, if only for a few minutes, to bring some new information and new life into your senses of sight, hearing, taste, smell, and touch.

MENTAL EXERCISES: Keep your mind active. Don't give yourself a chance to become a "couch potato." Mental exercises – puzzles or other games – keep the mind sharp, boost memory and reasoning abilities; whether it's cards, scrabble, or other word games.

A great way to improve your recall is to make a list, whether it's groceries, people you work – or worked – with, neighbors, or a to-do list and commit it to memory. An hour or so later, or even throughout the day, try to recall it and see how accurate you are.[44]

TRY USING YOUR NON-DOMINANT HAND THROUGHOUT THE DAY: This practice will certainly challenge your brain and mix up your everyday routine with a different perspective – and, according to studies, may even unleash some repressed emotions. Try using your non-dominant hand to: write, brush your teeth, open jars, butter your toast, wash your body, or use your computer mouse.[45]

FEELING: It's very important for the Rock to incorporate more vigorous movement into their daily activities. While one of their prized traits is to be more grounded than other people, they also have a tendency to slip into inactivity or lethargy. To restore and maintain balance, the Rock needs to be invigorated through physical exercise, enlivened through sound, and energized through the company of motivating people.

INCORPORATE STIMULATING MOVEMENT: What we eat first becomes fluid, which is absorbed into the blood. The plasma, the liquid portion of our blood, transports the micronutrients around our body through channels which have no pumping mechanism of their own. So, our plasma system, just like our lymphatic system, requires the activity of our muscles to move plasma throughout our body. Without exercise, the body becomes undernourished because the plasma is not circulating and delivering nutrients to the body tissues. Lack of exercise also causes increased appetite because the body is not receiving the nourishment it needs so it begins to crave more food.[46]

Stimulating physical movement and more vigorous exercise are great ways to energize the Rock. Physical activities like rock climbing, hiking, jumping rope, aerobics, tennis, or jogging are excellent choices. It's particularly important for the Rock to work up a sweat in order to clear blocked channels. Remember, the Earth Element is naturally dense and easily accumulates mass. These qualities show up in the Rock as their tendency to gain weight; pointing to yet another reason why physical exercise is so important for them.

LISTEN TO ENLIVENING MUSIC: Everything vibrates at its own frequency. The "sure and steady" Rock naturally tends to move at a slower pace than the other elements. The danger exists, however, when the Rock takes on more than they can handle, physically and emotionally. When they become weighed down trying to prop others up, or dig their heels in deeper to resist change, their pace begins to grind ever more slowly, leading the Rock into a "sure and steady" downward spiral.

In your effort to rebalance yourself, turn on the music! Get moving, and don't be shy about turning up the volume. For the Rock, the harder the beat and the louder the volume, the better. Go for music that energizes you. Go for music that has high tones. Go for music that will shake things up! Choose Rock for its contagious energy; Rap for its rapid, rhythmic lyrics; Latin for its vibrant rhythm; Opera because it is so engaging; or even Beethoven for the passion. Any one of these styles are great choices to help energize the Rock as you re-introduce movement and energy back into your life.

SEEK OUT MOTIVATING PEOPLE TO ASSOCIATE WITH: At the risk of becoming inactive and idle, you want to maintain good energy around you. Engaging in a stimulating conversation or spending time with someone you find exciting will take your mind off the "same old same old" and re-charge your feel-good emotions.

When you talk with someone you find motivating, it "steps up your game," it opens up ideas personally and professionally, it puts your mind and energy on something other than yourself, and it will likely inspire you to not "sit around" but to move forward with your plans and dreams.

EATING: Meals that are fresh and invigorating will definitely benefit the Rock. They will lighten up the physical and emotional load that the Rock tends to carry while still being nourishing and satisfying. You want to restore your steady energy and stamina, not be weighed down by it.

Steering clear of refined sugar will also go miles in restoring your balance. Adding pungent foods and spices to your diet are particularly beneficial to you as they stimulate digestion and improve your metabolism.[47]

Always consider: What kinds of raw materials am I using to rebuild and rejuvenate my body? Inferior raw materials will build an inferior structure, both physically and emotionally. Something won't be "plumb." It will be off-kilter.

EAT HIGH-QUALITY FOODS, YET LIGHTER IN DENSITY: Focus on preparing and eating fresh food that has the vitality of being alive or has been recently cooked. On an energetic level, you want to consume food that has life force or "prana" in it. That spark of energy in the food will translate into vitality in your body, mind, and spirit. It will *enliven* you. Eating fresh, whole, natural foods will cultivate a balanced alertness and feed you with sustained energy.

If you focus on eating fresh food that is full of readily available nutrients, like whole grains, freshly cooked vegetables, high quality protein, healthy fat, and fresh fruit, you will be feeding your organs what they demand and require. You'll be supplying your body with a full range of nutrients so you will feel satisfied after eating.

When we eat food that is void of nutrients, our body isn't satisfied. We develop cravings which cause us to search out *more* food, that's usually *inferior* in quality, in order to satisfy our hunger. Sugary treats and other artificially sweetened food and beverages fall into this category. They will temporarily make you feel full, but their effect will leave you right away without nourishing your body or your mind. In fact, you'll just continue to crave more of the same. When you eat "foods" that are not made from live, fresh ingredients, you won't feel alive or fresh either.

Avoid foods that have been chemically processed because they have no spark of life in them. Typically, they are made from refined and artificial ingredients which are designed to preserve, color, flavor, and give them texture. These foods are low in nutrients and fiber and are high in sugar and fat. Warmed-up food that was once frozen, microwaved food, and left-overs also fall into this "lifeless" category. They promote physical sluggishness and mental dullness. Your body will become larger, not necessarily stronger, from eating these types of foods, and your energy and vitality will surely and steadily decrease. They're not doing your health or your personality any favors!

Lighten up on the density of what you consume as well. Heavily textured foods you may want to consider steering clear of include beef, pork, bread, pastas, nut butters, deep-fried foods and rich desserts, like pudding, pies and cakes. Remember, you want to energize your body not weigh it down.

A meal of crisp, lightly steamed vegetables drizzled with a little sunflower oil and seasoned with your favorite herbs and spices is a great choice. Creative salads are a good "go to" for the Rock. Consider adding some grains like quinoa or couscous and plenty of brightly colored vegetables to a base of watercress, bok choy, or other leafy greens.

White meat of chicken or turkey, and freshwater fish are nourishing but won't weigh you down.

Healthy snacking includes puffed wheat and puffed rice because of their light quality. Popcorn is another great choice, perhaps sprinkled with some invigorating spices like ginger powder, turmeric powder, and/or cinnamon. Or sprinkle some freshly ground black pepper on top. Try using ghee instead of oil when making popcorn as it imparts a delicious buttery flavor, has a higher heat tolerance than common cooking oils, and is a healthier alternative to other fats.[48]

ADD VARIETY TO YOUR MEALS: I used to sit next to a guy at work whose daily consumption exclusively consisted of sugar in one form or another. He ate cookies – either store-bought or homemade – and drank soda-pop all day long. In the morning, he opened a bag of cookies and drank a can of Diet Coke. In the afternoon, he ate more cookies and drank a can of Dr. Pepper. I guess the change in soda was his version of "variety." Not only was Brian overweight, he had the dullest personality you can imagine.

I sat next to Brian for a couple of years. I was always the one to say "Good Morning," "Have a good evening" or to make any form of small talk throughout the day. The longest conversation I ever had with him was in the month of October one year. I distinctly remember asking him one morning what kind of cookies he was eating. He became as animated as I have ever seen him (and that wasn't much) as he proceeded to explain how the grocery stores were now carrying Halloween Oreos. To bolster his point, he opened his desk drawer and lifted out an open package. He pulled the flap back even more and proudly showed me all the different images that were embossed on his Oreo cookies: bats, haunted houses, laughing pumpkin faces, and smiling skeletons. I still laugh at the monotone way he said "here's a baaat" as he offered up Exhibit A for my approval. I don't know if my response convinced Brian or not, but I mustered up all the effort I could to share in his glee.

The Rock has a strong tendency keep things the same with little or no change. Don't let that happen with your meals! Don't eat the same things all the time. It's like getting stuck in a food rut. Mix things up with different colors (follow the rainbow), different textures (hard, soft, creamy, crunchy), and different directional growth (upward and out like lettuce, up and in like chives, down and out like beets, or down and in like carrots). Have it all! Bring your attention to your plate and put some planning into your meals.

INCORPORATE PUNGENT FOODS AND WARMING, INVIGORATING SPICES: Foods with the pungent taste are especially beneficial in keeping the excess Earth Element from accumulating in the Rock. Pungent foods stimulate digestion and metabolism, and improve circulation. They shake things up which, sometimes, is the perfect remedy for a sluggish Rock.

Sauté garlic and onions and add them to soups or cooked vegetables. Cut up radishes or turnips and include them in a salad. Expand your culinary repertoire.

Add warming herbs and spices to your meals like black peppercorns, curry powder, or horseradish. Chili pepper, cayenne, and oregano will certainly stimulate your body and mind when you find yourself in need of some motivation to change.

Mustard seed powder, turmeric, cumin and ginger is a great spice combination for soups and stews and will certainly move a tired Rock into action.

Conclusion:
The Answers Lie Within You

As you can see, nature completely provides for us on our journey through life. She gives us space to host our visions, the movement to create, the burning desire and intellect to transform, the fluidity to smooth over rough spots, and the strength to not just endure, but to enjoy the ride.

While we're bombarded with new exercise crazes, psychological jargon, and dietary advice, the problem is that you don't know if these latest trends in work-outs, buzzwords or fad diets will really work for you.

Following Nature's lead when it comes to understanding, regaining and maintaining your health is a far more sure-footed approach. The characteristics of the natural elements are reliable because their inherent qualities will never change: Space will always host, Air will always desire to flow, Fire will always be hot, Water will always be cohesive, and Earth will always be dense. This understanding is the beauty, and the key, to unlocking your unique nature and working with these inherent qualities to guide you on your path toward wellness.

The most important message I want you to take from this book is, when it comes to re-establishing your physical and emotional well-being, look inward for guidance rather than outward for a "fix." No matter what stage of life you find yourself in, it's never too late to discover the key that unlocks the secrets to your unique nature and natural inclinations.

Really assess how you're living your life and what you'd like to change. And trust that healthy, minor adjustments can make a world of difference both physically and emotionally, not only now, but well into the future. Simply put, you possess the potential to heal your body and your mind.

When you are in balance, you are a wellspring of ideas, you effortlessly bring them into form, you set them ablaze as you transform them into reality, you're nurturing to others and to yourself, and you have the strength to hold firm to your convictions. You radiate vibrant health. You have the power to realize your fullest potential and you can accomplish anything you set your intention on.

My very best advice? Follow the words of Rumi and take them to heart:

"EVERYTHING IN THE UNIVERSE IS WITHIN YOU. ASK ALL FROM YOURSELF."

FOOTNOTES

1. The First Trial, by Steven H. Goldberg, page 202.
2. Svoboda, Robert. Prakriti: Your Ayurvedic Constitution. Delhi: Motilal Banarsidass Publishers, 2005. Page 94
3. Watson, L Renee, Marianne Fraser, and Paul Ballas. "Journaling for Mental Health." Journaling for Mental Health - Health Encyclopedia - University of Rochester Medical Center. University of Rochester Medical Center. Accessed September 23, 2019. https://www.urmc.rochester.edu/encyclopedia/content.aspx?ContentID=4552&ContentTypeID=1.
4. Excerpt from Thoreau's Journal, October, 1853.
5. Stevenson, Shawn. "The Incredible Health Benefits of Walking Barefoot Daily." Benefits of Earthing: How Touching the Ground Improves Health. Conscious Lifestyle Magazine, April 25, 2019. https://www.consciouslifestylemag.com/earthing-and-grounding-benefits/.
6. Gagné Steve. Food Energetics: the Spiritual, Emotional, and Nutritional Power of What We Eat. Rochester, VT: Healing Arts Press, 2008. Page 109-111.
7. Gagné Steve. Food Energetics: the Spiritual, Emotional, and Nutritional Power of What We Eat. Rochester, VT: Healing Arts Press, 2008. Page 87.
8. Know Your Body: The Atlas of Anatomy. Berkeley, CA: Ulysses Press, 1995. Page 61.
9. Know Your Body: The Atlas of Anatomy. Berkeley, CA: Ulysses Press, 1995. Page 54.
10. Hanh Nhat, and Mobi Ho. The Miracle of Mindfulness: an Introduction to the Practice of Meditation. Boston: Beacon Press, 2016.
11. Novotny, Sarah, and Len Kravitz. "The Science of Breathing." The Science of Breathing. Accessed September 23, 2019. https://www.unm.edu/~lkravitz/Article folder/Breathing.html.
12. Halpern, Mark. "Ayurveda and Asana: Yoga Poses for Your Health." Yoga Journal, April 12, 2017. https://www.yogajournal.com/lifestyle/ayurveda-and-asana.
13. 101 Essential Tips: Yoga. Bolton, Ont.: Fenn Pub Co., 1995.
14. "Legs-Up-the-Wall (Viparita Karani)." Ayurveda Vata-Pacifying Yoga: Legs Up the Wall | Banyan Botanicals. Accessed September 23, 2019. https://www.banyanbotanicals.com/info/ayurvedic-living/living-ayurveda/yoga/vata-pacifying-yoga/vata-yoga-poses-legs-up-the-wall/.

15. Greshko, Michael. "The Sun, Explained." Our solar system: The sun information and facts, January 4, 2019. https://www.nationalgeographic.com/science/space/solar-system/the-sun/.
16. Lepore, Donald. "The Ultimate Healing System": Breakthrough in Nutrition, Kinesiology and Holistic Healing Techniques. Provo, UT: Woodland Books, 1988.
17. Greshko, Michael. "The Sun, Explained." Our solar system: The sun information and facts, January 4, 2019. https://www.nationalgeographic.com/science/space/solar-system/the-sun/.
18. "Phoenix (Mythology)." Phoenix (mythology) - New World Encyclopedia. Accessed September 23, 2019. https://www.newworldencyclopedia.org/entry/Phoenix_(mythology).
19. Sarkis, Stephanie. "Watching Violent News Video Can Be Hazardous to Your Health." Psychology Today. Sussex Publishers. Accessed September 23, 2019. https://www.psychologytoday.com/us/blog/here-there-and-everywhere/201710/watching-violent-news-video-can-be-hazardous-your-health.
20. Scott, Elizabeth. "How Noise Pollution Might Be Stressing You Out." Verywell Mind. Verywell Mind, July 16, 2018. https://www.verywellmind.com/stress-and-noise-pollution-how-you-may-be-at-risk-3145041.
21. Know Your Body: The Atlas of Anatomy. Berkeley, CA: Ulysses Press, 1995. Pages 57-58.
22. Morter, M. T. Your Health Your Choice. Hollywood: Frederick Fell, 2015. Pages 226-227.
23. Kshirsagar, Manisha, and Megan M. Murphy. Enchanting Beauty: Ancient Secrets to Inner, Outer & Lasting Beauty. Twin Lakes, WI: Lotus Press, 2015. Pages 144-149.
24. Dembling, Sophia. "Introspection Versus Rumination." Psychology Today. Sussex Publishers. Accessed September 23, 2019. https://www.psychologytoday.com/us/blog/the-introverts-corner/201302/introspection-versus-rumination.
25. Chopra, Deepak. Perfect Health: the Complete Mind Body Guide. London: Royal National Institute for the Blind, 2006. Page 295.
26. Ballentine, Rudolph. Diet and Nutrition: a Holistic Approach. Honesdale, Pa: Himalayan International Institute, 1979. Pages 308-309.
27. Morter, M. T. Your Health Your Choice. Hollywood: Frederick Fell, 2015. Pages 82-84.
28. Atreya, Vaidya. Ayurvedic Nutrition. U.S.A.: Avery Pub., 2010. Page 55.

29. "Amniotic Fluid." March of Dimes, June 2013. https://www.marchofdimes.org/pregnancy/amniotic-fluid.aspx.
30. Water Q&A: Why is water the "universal solvent"? Accessed September 23, 2019. https://water.usgs.gov/edu/qa-solvent.html.
31. "Water Birth: Benefits and Potential Risks." American Pregnancy Association, July 16, 2019. https://americanpregnancy.org/labor-and-birth/water-birth/.
32. Know Your Body: The Atlas of Anatomy. Berkeley, CA: Ulysses Press, 1995. Pages 17.
33. Know Your Body: The Atlas of Anatomy. Berkeley, CA: Ulysses Press, 1995. Page 21.
34. Lopez, Gerry. "Inside the Tube." The Inertia, December 7, 2011. https://www.theinertia.com/surf/inside-the-tube/.
35. "Tsunamis: Facts About Killer Waves." National Geographic, August 15, 2018. https://www.nationalgeographic.com/news/2005/1/tsunamis-facts-about-killer-waves/.
36. Know Your Body: The Atlas of Anatomy. Berkeley, CA: Ulysses Press, 1995. Page 106.
37. McCaffrey, Patrick. "The Meninges and Cerebrospinal Fluid." Detailed Information: The Meninges and Cerebrospinal Fluid. Accessed September 23, 2019. https://www.csuchico.edu/~pmccaffrey//syllabi/CMSD 320/362unit3.html.
38. Know Your Body: The Atlas of Anatomy. Berkeley, CA: Ulysses Press, 1995. Page 30.
39. Simon, Harvey B. "Giving Thanks Can Make You Happier." Harvard Health. Accessed September 23, 2019. https://www.health.harvard.edu/healthbeat/giving-thanks-can-make-you-happier.
40. "Making North America: Granite vs. Basalt Formation." PBS LearningMedia. NOVA, August 31, 2019. https://www.pbslearningmedia.org/resource/nvmn-sci-granitebasalt/wgbh-nova-making-north-america-granite-vs-basalt-formation/.
41. "Earth's Interior." National Geographic, January 18, 2017. https://www.nationalgeographic.com/science/earth/surface-of-the-earth/earths-interior/.
42. "Landslide Hazards--A National Threat." USGS Science for a Changing World, December 2005. https://pubs.usgs.gov/fs/2005/3156/2005-3156.pdf.
43. American Bone Health. "Minerals for Bone Health." American Bone

Health, June 18, 2019. https://americanbonehealth.org/nutrition/minerals-for-bone-health/.

44. Harvard Health Publishing. "6 Simple Steps to Keep Your Mind Sharp at Any Age." Harvard Health. Accessed September 23, 2019. https://www.health.harvard.edu/mind-and-mood/6-simple-steps-to-keep-your-mind-sharp-at-any-age.

45. Rose, Jeff. "The Benefits of Using Your Opposite Hand: Grow Brain Cells." Good Financial Cents®, April 1, 2019. https://www.goodfinancialcents.com/benefits-of-using-your-opposite-hand-grow-brain-cells-while-brushing-your-teeth/.

46. Chandler, Stephanie. "Blood Plasma Functions." LIVESTRONG.COM. Leaf Group. Accessed September 23, 2019. https://www.livestrong.com/article/107577-blood-plasma-functions/.

47. Atreya, Vaidya. Ayurvedic Nutrition. U.S.A.: Avery Pub., 2010. Page 55.

48. Staughton, John. "7 Impressive Benefits of Ghee (Clarified Butter)." Organic Facts, February 20, 2019. https://www.organicfacts.net/health-benefits/other/ghee-clarified-butter.html.

49. The Five Elements in Ayurvedic Medicine | CA College of Ayurveda, California College of Ayurveda, 2019, www.ayurvedacollege.com/articles/five-elements-ayurvedic-medicine.

www.ingramcontent.com/pod-product-compliance
Lightning Source LLC
Chambersburg PA
CBHW021956290426
44108CB00012B/1097